Marketing Metrics and Financial Performance

Conclusions 47

Measures Used in Practice 47
Toward a Common Metric Chain 47
Open Issues 49
Growth: The Ultimate Metric? 49
Summary 51

References 55
For Further Reading 69
About the Authors 75
About MSI 77
Related MSI Working Papers 79

Figure

Figure 1. The Structure of Metrics: From Marketing to Market Cap 9

Tables

Table 1. Customer Metrics 12
Table 2. Brand/Product Metrics 12
Table 3. Financial Metrics 13
Table 4. Marketing Mix Metrics 14
Table 5. Web Metrics and Source of Information 16
Table 6. Key Metrics by Industry 17
Table 7. Perspectives on Brand Equity 36
Table 8. Sources of Business Margin by Brand and Customer 37
Table 9. Percent of Firms Reporting Metric to Board 48
Table 10. Current State of Knowledge 50

Foreword

We are pleased to present *Marketing Metrics and Financial Performance,* by former MSI Executive Directors Donald Lehmann and David Reibstein, the fifth book in the MSI Relevant Knowledge Series. MSI has been a leader in encouraging, funding, and disseminating research on marketing metrics for the past decade. Lehmann and Reibstein's book provides a readable and actionable summary of the key findings in this stream of research.

Lehmann and Reibstein's approach to metrics is aimed at *making marketing matter*. They first describe the menu of marketing metrics available to practitioners, and the relative merits of each. They then make the all-important connection between marketing actions, customer assets, and business performance, not only in traditional product markets, but also in financial markets. Last, but not least, they offer important guidance on the different research methods that may be used to quantify these connections. In an age of unprecedented emphasis on marketing accountability, Lehmann and Reibstein's monograph is a must-read.

Dominique M. Hanssens
UCLA
MSI Executive Director

Executive Summary

Attention to the financial impact of marketing actions is not new, but global competition, recession, and stock market pressure have increased the push for marketing accountability. Further, the large and increasing portion of shareholder value (market capitalization) that is seen as attributable to "intangible" assets such as customers and brands has strengthened the need to link marketing expenditures to financial outcomes.

A "value chain" provides a basis for modeling marketing productivity. In this chain, company actions—such as R&D, advertising spending, and customer targeting—impact the mindset of customers, employees, partners, and competitors. Customers' mindsets (attitudes) then drive their behavior in the product-markets, which produces sales and profits. Finally, at least for public companies, financial performance (sales, profits) determines stock price and market capitalization.

Marketing metrics need to demonstrate the productivity of marketing actions and spending in relation to this ultimate goal of stock price, yet few actions have a pronounced direct effect on stock price. For this reason, intermediate goals are often utilized. These include customer metrics, brand metrics, financial performance metrics, marketing mix metrics, and Web metrics.

Linking to Product-Market Performance

Marketing Mix   Empirical work on the impact of advertising on sales has shown some consistent findings. Ad spending on a mature product has little short-term impact on sales, while ad spending on a new product, or a new use of an old product, has a measurable and nontrivial effect. Research on the effect of promotions suggests that they have a positive short-term and negative long-term impact with the total effect positive (in the absence of competitive reactions).

Substantial research has also investigated interactions between marketing mix variables, particularly advertising's impact on prices. Some research suggests that advertising allows a firm to charge a higher price by creating greater demand. Other research shows the opposite: as advertising increases, competition intensifies, thereby lowering prices to the customer.

Marketing Capabilities and Strategy There is substantial work on the impact of brand equity on product-market outcomes. Generally, brand equity reduces sensitivity to price increases and makes advertising more effective as well as directly creates a "revenue premium" for the firm.

There is a vast literature on metrics related to new products, much of it focused on development. Considerable effort addresses the pattern of product diffusion. Much of this uses the Bass (1969) model and suggests that innovation is fairly rare for consumer durables, that there is a lag between introduction and takeoff of several years, and that patterns vary by country. The impact of new product entry order on sales has also been extensively studied, and most studies find an advantage to early entry.

There has been some investigation of the impact of increasing the firm's product line. For example, as a firm extends its product line upward, its brand's equity increases (although extending the brand upward may make it difficult to sell the product). Conversely, when a firm extends its brand downward, brand equity decreases, although it is easier to sell the lower-end offering.

Market Orientation Market orientation has generally been positively linked to market performance, although its impact depends on market conditions. Being entrepreneurial and market-oriented have been shown to positively impact performance. Further, meta-analysis to assess the impact of market orientation finds a positive relationship with product-market results, especially for manufacturing (versus service) firms.

Linking to Financial Performance/Stock Value

Marketing Mix Overall, research linking advertising spending to stock performance concludes that advertising contributes significantly to the stock performance of non-manufacturing (but not manufacturing) firms. Research assessing the impact of promotions finds they do not increase long-term financial performance.

The impact of new product announcements and introductions has been studied fairly extensively. While new product announcements appear to increase stock price, delays in new product introductions decrease it.

Research examining the impact of reductions in expenditures to improve current earnings prior to equity offerings finds that firms that cut expenditures prior to offerings tend to have lower long-term stock performance.

Marketing Strategy Linking marketing strategy to financial performance has a long history beginning with the Profit Impact of Marketing Strategy (PIMS) project in 1972.

Interestingly, it appears that firms that employ an umbrella (corporate) brand are valued by the stock market more highly than firms with multiple brands; that some firms are better off increasing value appropriation while others can improve by specializing in either value creation or value appropriating; and that adding Internet channels has a positive impact, especially for strong companies and early followers.

Brand quality and attitude both relate to stock value. Not surprisingly, therefore, changing a brand name also has a significant financial impact.

Marketing Assets

Satisfaction Customer satisfaction is linked to product-market results via repeat purchase rates and favorable word-of-mouth. Satisfaction is the key metric for predicting retention and, hence, customer lifetime value (CLV) and firm value. Importantly, there is evidence that satisfaction relates to firm return on assets (ROA), and that satisfaction not only increases average returns but also lowers risk (variance). Satisfaction measures based on the American Consumer Satisfaction Index have been linked to three product-market measures (sales, margin, share) and three financial measures (Tobin's q, cash flow, shareholder return).

Customers Managing customers as assets is now an accepted concept in marketing. The basic metric in this area is customer lifetime value, which considers the long-run buying behavior of a customer. The value of customers is the expected discounted cash flow from customers in the future. It depends on three components: acquisition (rate and cost), retention (rate and cost), and expansion/growth in same customer margin (amount and cost).

The leverage a firm gets from increasing retention appears to be the greatest of the three components: retention has more marginal impact on CLV than either acquisition cost or the discount rate. However, maximizing retention probably means "leaving money on the table." Not only does it ignore the fact that some customers are not profitable but, as with satisfaction, it is easier to maximize by focusing on a small segment of customers.

Brands Brands represent a significant fraction of the intangible, and hence, total, value of many firms. A key issue is how to estimate brand value in a consistent manner. This raises two critical questions. The first is conceptual: Does brand equity refer to the value of the brand to the customer or the value of the brand to the firm (aggregated across customers)? Typically, those in the marketing function take the customer-centric view, while those higher in the organization or outside marketing take the firm view. The second question is whether brand equity can be captured by a single measure. In practice, brand metrics vary widely.

Unfortunately, there has been little research into what a firm needs to spend in order to either create or maintain brand equity. Similarly, we know little about how quickly a brand's equity erodes. Both of these are vital for determining the value of marketing spending.

Methodological Approaches and Issues

Cross-sectional versus Time-Series Data Time-series data allow for testing the impact of marketing over time. They also raise the issue of whether an effect lasts one period or a few periods (a.k.a. the "dust-settling" period), or is permanent. The choice of cross-sectional versus time-series data (as well as the level of aggregation) also impacts the results.

The Impact of Competition   That competition reaction occurs is well established; less well known is when and how competitors react. Some work suggests that competitors react immediately to a firm's actions regardless of the impact; other work suggests that firms only react if their own performance is affected, or if the competition firm's actions reap positive results. The timing and strength of competitive reaction is important in assessing the overall impact of any marketing action.

Subjective versus Objective Performance Measures   Objective measures such as sales or profits are comparable across, as well as within, industries. However, subjective measures are often employed for reasons of convenience and availability. Future research is needed to calibrate the effect of using subjective measures on links in the value chain.

Statistical Methods   These include persistence modeling (to assess the impact of marketing actions on product-market performance), event studies (when a marketing activity is a discrete event significant enough to have a measurable impact on stock value), stock market modeling (an econometric regression-like procedure), and meta-analysis. The last, meta-analysis, appears to be an excellent way to establish typical measures of the strength of the various links in the chain as well as to uncover important systematic variance in the strength of links.

Comprehensive Testing   There are two approaches to comprehensively examining the metrics value chain. The first is to collect data on all the components for a sample of companies and analyze the results in a multiple equation model. The second is to piece together links as is sometimes done in meta-analyses in the management area. This involves some technical issues (for example, the correlations may be impacted by peculiar conditions of the study from which they are taken).

Estimating Effects and Action Optimization   Marketers are interested in optimizing marketing activities and budgets. One approach is to develop reduced-form models that link firm actions directly to stock price. Unfortunately, many marketing actions are not likely to produce a measurable change in the stock price. Even if the link is clear, the reduced-form model provides little diagnostic information as to the process or timeline by which results emerge.

Another approach is to separately estimate direct links in the metric value chain. The total effect is estimated by multiplying through the links in the chain (as in path analysis). Unfortunately, the variance of a product is the product of the variances, each of which is large at this stage of knowledge development. The result is high uncertainty about impacts.

Timing of Effects The accounting practice of expensing marketing expenditures results in an assessment of marketing's impact in the period in which the expenditures occur. Yet, it is well established that many marketing activities have important long-run impacts (that is, their effects may be enduring). Evaluating marketing in its current-period impact will lead to underestimating its true value.

Conclusion

Conceptually, it is useful to think of a metrics value chain as the key tool for monitoring marketing actions. Practically, however, it is difficult to estimate all the links in such a chain in a given situation. Other approaches (i.e., meta-analysis, judgment) may help estimate the links in a particular case, and simulation can be done to capture variance in outcomes. Making explicit the judgments on these links makes the assumptions visible to others, subject to being challenged and, when they pass scrutiny, available for use in other situations.

Overall, several important findings emerge from research on marketing productivity:

- Retention drives CLV.

- CLV drives stock value.

- Satisfaction drives retention (and therefore CLV) and stock value.

- New products enhance stock value.

Where are we in terms of generating empirical generalizations about the numerical size of the various links? While studies have generated parameter estimates for the strength of some links in the metric value chain, many others are lacking. In addition, most of the estimates available are based on linking two of the elements only, the equivalent of simple correlations. This under-specification leads to potential problems and biases in the results. Thus, in addition to more studies linking particular elements in the chain, comprehensive studies are needed that estimate the entire chain in a multi-equation model framework.

Introduction

For the past several years a top-tier research priority of the Marketing Science Institute has been marketing metrics. With economic downturns, there has been pressure throughout the organization for every unit to justify its budget. While marketing is not an exception, historically marketing has not demonstrated a direct link to the financial statement. This monograph begins by briefly reviewing the reasons behind the pressure for "accountability." We next describe a metrics value chain which captures the various levels of measurement involved. We then discuss evidence for the various links in the chain. Problems in establishing the links are discussed and suggestions for future work offered.

Donald R. Lehmann
David J. Reibstein

"You can't manage what you don't measure."
—W. Edwards Deming

Knowledge without quantification is of a
"meagre and unsatisfactory kind."

"To measure is to know."

"If you can not measure it, you can not improve it."
—Lord Kelvin

"Not everything that can be measured is important and not everything that is important can be measured."
—Albert Einstein

The Metrics Imperative: Making Marketing Matter

The current push within marketing for metrics that demonstrate marketing's productivity has finally caught up with calls that have been voiced largely from outside the field (e.g., Kirpalani and Shapiro 1973). Specifically, CEOs and CFOs, spurred by global competition, recession, and stock market pressure to deliver "the numbers," have shown an increasing tendency to question—and cut—marketing budgets. Marketing's limited ability to demonstrate its direct impact on the firm's financial performance has made it easy to reduce marketing spending without explicitly recognizing negative impacts of the reduction. Consequently, these reductions in marketing budgets have caught marketers' attention and strengthened the imperative to connect marketing spending to the financial impact on the firm.

The response by some in the marketing profession has been less than enthusiastic, falling back on arguments which are essentially nihilistic (i.e., it can't be done, or at least done precisely, so why bother) or, in the case of many, at least in academia, deciding it is not their problem. Still, several scholars have advocated better metrics.

Concern about the financial impact of marketing actions is not entirely new. The Profit Impact of Marketing Strategy (PIMS) project, begun in 1972, was a survey-based attempt to assess the impact of marketing across companies and industries. Much of this work is summarized by Buzzell and Gale (1987) and is more recently re-assessed in a book edited by Farris and Moore (2004). While a major thrust of the work was assessing the profit impact of market share, other topics such as product quality and new products were also considered. Since much of the data were disguised (due to confidentiality concerns), the results were directional and relative, but not directly calibrated to "real" dollar results.

A seminal piece in this area is the award-winning article by Srivastava, Shervani, and Fahey (1998) that connects marketing assets to stockholder value. In addition, since 1997 the Marketing Science Institute (MSI) has identified metrics and marketing productivity as top research priorities, based on its biennial survey of member companies. Interestingly, financial markets have also begun to recognize that firm valuations are more dependent on "intangible assets." The large and increasing fraction of shareholder value (market capitalization) or market-to-book ratio that is seen as attributable to intangible assets such as customers and brands has added further impetus to the drive to better-justify marketing expenditures.

Of course, not all firms are concerned with maximizing stock value. Privately held firms may be more concerned with maintaining a steady stream of income or preparing for an IPO. Other firm goals include short-term cash flow and obtaining "hard" currency. Moreover, nonprofit institutions have other goals, for example, expanding the number who receive treatment for a particular condition and/or adhere to it, maintaining and expanding membership, impacting society, or even the fuzzy but lofty goal of creating and disseminating knowledge.

While nonprofits, etc., are important, this monograph focuses on for-profit firms which are publicly held or whose objectives can be defined in terms of product-market results and, ultimately, stock price. Of course, this ignores numerous other stakeholders, including the community where business is conducted and society as a whole. How much these should be considered is the matter of some debate. Since adequately dealing with these other parties is a major task in its own right, however, here we focus on stock price as the ultimate goal.

However, stock price is not always operationally useful either as a performance indicator or diagnostically. Few actions (e.g., a single ad, promotion, or line extension) have a pronounced direct effect on stock price. While a general strategy or policy (e.g., an emphasis on new products) may impact stock price, at least across companies, the impacts of most individual marketing decisions are limited. For that reason, intermediate goals are utilized. The problem with doing this is two-fold. First, the intermediate goals used have often been far removed from stock price (e.g., awareness). It is hard to justify any expenditure if it does not ultimately help increase the stock price or the cash flow. Moreover, these criteria have differed across marketing decisions (e.g., awareness and attitude to the ad and the product for advertising versus the immediate increase in sales from a promotion), making it difficult to compare, say, advertising and promotion effectiveness. Thus, at a minimum there is a need to calibrate effectiveness across measures.

Firms and individual researchers often focus on results that apply to a very narrow range of situations (i.e., a single company in a single product category). Developing a situation-specific value chain is indeed a worthwhile activity, and collecting data at the brand level is consistent with what market research firms typically do. However, in the Bayesian tradition, such results are inefficient since they ignore related information (that is, learning in one category, such as paper towels, is not used to enhance learning in another category, such as paper napkins), thereby overlooking some important similarities and inter-dependencies. Since the purpose of this monograph is general, we focus on studies that cover multiple products/services and the development of a general metrics value chain.

Types of Marketing Metrics

Marketing does not lack metrics (Ambler 2003). Rather, marketing lacks a structure for organizing and relating these metrics. Most metrics can be distinguished along three dimensions.

Diagnostic versus Evaluative Diagnostic metrics are intended to help understand where a firm (product, brand) stands and how it got there. An excellent example is customer attitude, which explains why customers do, or do not, buy. Many brand equity measures fall into this category as does (price and volume) variance accounting.

By contrast, evaluative metrics are used for performance appraisal, for example, "What were the resulting sales?" "Show me the money," and "Just tell me if you won or lost." Essentially these are the type of metrics a CEO or CFO relies on as well as managers with responsibility for overall profitability. For example, a sales manager cares mainly about the sales generated by the sales staff, not the number of sales calls.

Short versus Long Term Metrics have a time dimension. Some capture the immediate or short-term results ("deliverables") of marketing such as awareness for ads and a sales bump (increase) for consumer promotions. Short-term metrics are generally used by constituencies within the firm, usually within the marketing department. Immediate goals can be diagnostic (e.g., ad recall was low) and evaluative (e.g., Was low recall due to copy or media plan? Did the ad reach its target audience?).

Other measures are long term and thus forward looking, and are used by managers to assess future planning. While describing the current situation (e.g., sales in District A) is useful, knowing where things are headed is critical. Hence, the pattern of changes in descriptive measures becomes relevant. In addition, some descriptive measures turn out to be predictive of future results. (We discuss one of these, satisfaction, in some detail later.)

Forward-looking measures focus on impact over time. For example, one might evaluate an advertising campaign by looking not only at awareness (an immediate consequence) but also at impact on sales (performance), and next year's awareness or brand equity (forward-looking). Systems thinkers, such as Steve Haeckel, formerly of IBM, argue that the appropriate metrics for an action (e.g., ad, promotion) are the controllable consequences it generates (awareness, amount bought on promotion) which may or may not be easy to link to firm goals (e.g., profits) due to a number of external factors (e.g., competition).

Level in the Organization For constituencies at the top of, or outside, the firm, financial performance measures such as return on investment (ROI) and cash flow, as well as the "ultimate" metrics for publicly traded firms—stock price and market capitalization—are critical. These metrics are mainly the derivatives of the immediate (short-term) results. For example, a salesman may have goals (and hence metrics) in terms of call frequency. The VP of sales, by contrast, may look at call frequency as diagnostic of performance, but has an overall sales goal. The CFO, in turn, is likely to be more concerned with profits and treat variation in sales from goal as diagnostic.

Given these distinctions, it is important to indicate the primary focus of this monograph. Put simply, we concentrate most of our efforts on linking marketing to evaluative, final goals of the "boss"—in this case, the CFO, COO, or CEO. We do this for two reasons. First, the marketing literature is largely populated with studies focusing on diagnostic, immediate goals of individuals below the top of the organization, making it impossible to give a reasonable summary of this work in limited space. Second, we would like to see marketing matter outside of marketing, i.e., to the firm as a whole. For these reasons we concentrate on linking the short-term and long-term effects of marketing and its assets (brands, customers) to financial performance and firm valuation.

Structuring Marketing Metrics

One way to track the myriad interim marketing measures is to develop a marketing "scorecard" (Kaplan and Norton 1996). Here, the measures all have value to someone in or outside the organization. Second, by using a system such as colors (green is good, red is bad) it is possible to get a general impression of how things are going. However, scorecards have three major shortcomings. Even with clever presentation, scorecards can be a bit overwhelming. Further, since changes in indicators such as customer satisfaction are critical, they need to contain not just level but also change measures, making them relatively complex. Finally, and most critically, scorecards often do not identify what drives what, much less indicate the impact of one variable on the others.

Reibstein et al. (2005) describe dashboards as the next evolution of the scorecard and identify five stages of dashboard development: (1) identification of the key metrics, (2) populating the dashboard with data, (3) establishing relationships between the dashboard items, (4) forecasting and doing "what if" analysis, and (5) connecting to financial consequences. From their perspective, a complete dashboard should be a set of metrics visible to the user that provides a snapshot of current status or performance of the business that is widely shared so that everyone involved can view the business in the same light. This is what we commonly see in dashboards that are color coded to reflect the current health of the industry. However, Reibstein et al. (2005) argue that for a dashboard to be complete, it must also include a set of inputs, generally marketing spending, as well as output measures. These outputs are financial performance metrics, such as sales and profits. In addition, a dashboard should integrate the impact of marketing spending on the interim marketing metrics and their impact on the financial consequences. Further, it should show both the short-term as well as the long-term impact, i.e., a dashboard should be not only historical but forward looking. Most corporate dashboards have not yet advanced to this stage (Reibstein et al. 2005).

For these reasons, many practitioners and academics are interested instead in capturing the links in a "value chain." We organize this discussion in terms of a metrics hierarchy/causal chain.

A number of authors have developed models of how various metrics link together. These include the service profit chain (Heskett et al. 1994; Kamakura et al. 2002), the brand value chain (Keller and Lehmann 2005), and the chain of marketing productivity (Rust, Lemon, and Zeithaml 2004) as well as the models presented by Srivastava, Shervani, and Fahey (1998), and Lehmann (2004). Based on these, Figure 1 presents a framework linking company actions with product-market and financial performance. Note it is incomplete. First, it does not explicitly include exogenous factors, such as the economy, which can have a massive impact on the metrics. Second, it does not explicitly incorporate feedback loops, such as from results to marketing actions. Nonetheless, it provides a useful framework for organizing our discussion.

The goal, then, is to establish the strength of the links so that even when not all measures are available, one can estimate the impact of marketing actions. A value chain ("flowboard") similar to Figure 1 provides the basis for such a model.

The first level of the chain consists of actions of the company, competitors, and industry and the environment in general. Of particular interest are company actions, the decision variables available to a firm (e.g., R&D and advertising spending, customer targeting).

The first impact of these activities is on the mindset of customers, employees, partners, etc., as well as on competitors, as indicated by reaction functions. For example, the main customer concern of P&G and Colgate may be the reaction of Wal-Mart. In any event, the impact on customers (current and potential) is critical. This leads to the use of measures of awareness (knowledge), associations (both product attribute and image based), attitude, and attachment/loyalty.

Figure 1
The Structure of Metrics: From Marketing to Market Cap

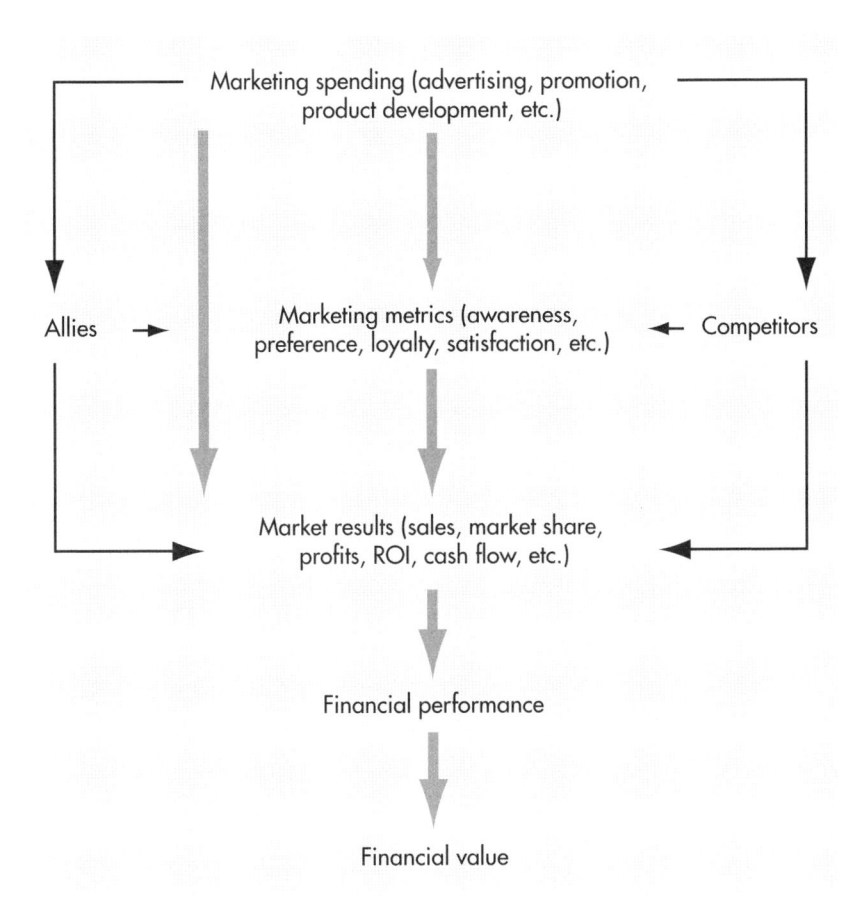

```
              Marketing spending (advertising, promotion,
                     product development, etc.)
                              │
                              ▼
 Allies →    Marketing metrics (awareness,    ← Competitors
             preference, loyalty, satisfaction, etc.)
                              │
                              ▼
       →     Market results (sales, market share,    ←
                 profits, ROI, cash flow, etc.)
                              │
                              ▼
                     Financial performance
                              │
                              ▼
                       Financial value
```

The next level involves customer behavior (versus mindset) in the product market. At the aggregate level this includes sales, share, average price paid, share of wallet, etc., as well as response sensitivities such as own- and cross-price elasticities.

The consequence of product market outcomes is financial performance. Measures such as net profit, ROI, and ROA (return on assets) as well as EVA (economic value added—net profit adjusted for the opportunity cost of capital tied up in the business) fall in this category.

The final level is the ultimate objective, stock price or variations of it such as MVA (market value added—change in market capitalization) or Tobin's q (stock price divided by book value with some adjustments).

Different people typically focus on different levels in this value chain, as illustrated below.

Level of Metric	Constituents
Customer mindset	Marketing specialists (advertising, promotion, product development)
Product-market performance	Product managers, CMOs
Financial performance	CMOs, CFOs
Firm valuation	CFOs, CEOs

For example, someone trying to fine-tune a promotion decision for one of many products rightly spends little time worrying about stock price. Similarly, someone charged with business unit or corporate results has little time to focus on diagnostic measures of consumer thinking. Rather they concentrate on profit and ROI. This leads, unfortunately, to the business equivalent of the Tower of Babel, with different parts of the organization speaking different languages. For example, it is difficult to gain budget approval for an expenditure that affects customer mindset if it is not clear that and how its impact flows ultimately to shareholder value.

A Metrics Menu

There are an essentially infinite number of metrics and variations on them. Here we discuss some of the most common metrics (and their variations) that are potentially relevant to marketing. (For complete definitions, underlying assumptions, and how to measure and use the metrics listed below, see Farris et al. (2006) in *Marketing Metrics: 50+ Metrics Every Executive Should Master.*)

As suggested earlier, what needs to be measured follows a natural progression from customer perceptions to product-market performance, financial returns, the value of marketing assets, and eventually stock market value. The first two categories, customer and product-market measures, are primarily used as diagnostic tools (to see how you are doing in terms of sales, etc., and why you are getting those results). The next category, financial performance metrics, is the key for performance assessment (i.e., Are you doing well enough?). For a publicly traded company, market capitalization is the gold standard in spite of recent irregularities. While the link from most products to market cap is hard to estimate, and product managers rarely even try, recognizing what the standard is helps focus efforts and facilitate communication within the organization.

Customer Metrics An excellent summary of customer metrics in general and satisfaction metrics in particular is provided by Gupta and Zeithaml (2006). Table 1 lists customer-based metrics, some of which are particularly useful in understanding a firm's performance. For example, "share of generic competition" goes beyond the normal definition of market share. A product manager for Discover Card might consider their competition to include department store cards, debit cards, American Express cards that do not permit revolving balances, and cash. Thus, "share of wallet" would be an indicator of the percentage of times the Discover Card is used for any payment.

Trial and repeat are relevant for new products because a new product will rarely be successful unless a sufficient number of households or companies try it and a significant number of them repeat (i.e., become long-term customers). Lifetime customer value can be used to place a value on a company such as Amazon. Customer defections signal possible weaknesses in the product line or aspects of the marketing strategy. Satisfaction is a particularly important measure, although overreliance on it can lead to nonoptimal decisions (i.e., having a small number of ecstatic customers).

Brand/Product Metrics A key group of metrics is designed to measure brand/product equity or strength. One set focuses on estimating brand equity or the perceived value of a brand. Young & Rubicam has its own proprietary measure as do Research International, Landor Associates, Millward Brown, and others. Brand strength can also be estimated using the price premium obtainable in the market relative to a competitor. Brand "health" (Bhattacharya and Lodish 1999) can be thought of as a

Table 1
Customer Metrics

Mindset	**Product-Market Behavior**
Awareness	Acquisition rate and cost
Associations	Complaints
Attitude	Customer lifetime value (CLV)
Attachment (loyalty)	Frequency
Activity (word of mouth)	Level of business/amount spent (expansion)
Consideration set	Recency
Intentions	Retention rate and cost
Satisfaction	Retention/repeat rate
Willingness to pay	Share of generic competition
Willingness to recommend	Trial/acquisition

combination of the current "well-being" of a brand (e.g., its market share) and its resistance to "disease," such as how loyal its customer base is to a promotional onslaught by a competitor. A list of brand/product metrics can be found in Table 2.

Among brand/product metrics, two predominate: sales and share. These "top-line" measures were for a long time the goal of marketing (i.e., before the current emphasis on profits and profitable growth).

Table 2
Brand/Product Metrics

Brand equity	Profit/margin
Brand "health"	Repeat purchase rate
Growth rate	Revenue premium
Number of customers	Share (of market, requirements, wallet)
Price premium	Unit sales/share

Financial Performance Metrics Financial performance metrics (Table 3) range from sales revenue to profits, margin, ROI/ROA, net present value (NPV), cash flow, marketing investment, stock returns (MVA), and Tobin's q. These are the critical results for most budget evaluations. Put bluntly: no profits, no approval.

There are serious questions about the usefulness of measures such as ROI or ROA. In addition to being backward-looking (i.e., historical), they encourage cost-cutting in weak economic times which may in fact be the best time to capture share and customers and hence drive long-run profitability (Srinivasan, Rangaswamy, and Lilien 2005). Similarly, ROI calculations tend to place a low value on growth options which have significant start-up costs. Moreover, it may be R – I, return minus investment (i.e., EVA), not ROI, that drives stock price.

Table 3
Financial Metrics

Economic value added (EVA)
Margins
Marketing investment
Profit
Return on investments/return on assets (ROI/ROA)
Sales
Stock returns (MVA)
Tobin's q

Marketing Mix Metrics Each of the program elements has its own direct outcomes that in turn lead to customer, product-marketing, and financial results. Some measures used by product managers to track and evaluate the marketing mix are shown in Table 4. Of course, costs are also needed to assess net, versus gross, impact.

Typically, product managers measure the effectiveness of advertising via awareness, recall, change in attitudes, and incremental sales. The first three are usually measured using either commercial or company-sponsored surveys. Incremental sales represent the gap between observed sales and what sales would have been without either the change in advertising copy or increase in spending. Incremental sales analyses can be conducted using internal sales and advertising data. Calculating advertising elasticities, the percentage change in sales due to a 1% change in advertising, requires statistical analysis of sales and price data.

In addition to sales response and awareness/recall attitude measures, product managers often measure advertising by traditional media

Table 4
Marketing Mix Metrics

Advertising
Awareness
Attitude toward ad
Attitude toward brand/product
Brand image
Elasticity
Incremental sales
Lead generation
Media (gross rating points, share of voice)
Recall
ROI

Promotion
Incremental sales
Long-term versus short-term
Repeat
ROI
Trial

Distribution and Place
Channel support (spending)
Cost
Facings
Number of distributors
Sales per store/stockkeeping units (SKU)
Distribution coverage (ACV)
Sales per (outlet, facing, . . .)
Strength of channel relationship

Price
Percentage on deal
Average customer price
Average deal percentage
Elasticity
Price
Price to trade
Relative price

Salesforce
Productivity (effort)
Sales versus goals
Customer satisfaction
Won/lost

Customer Service
Time to service
Percentage resolved on first try
Perceived performance

Product
Quality

---

measures which do not measure customer response, including gross rating points (GRPs), which are a combination of reach (number of people reached by the advertising) multiplied by frequency (the average number of exposures), and share of voice (SOV) spending relative to competition which is often compared to market share. The data necessary for these metrics are usually collected by commercial firms specializing in tracking media such as Competitive Media Reporting.

Some companies track the average size and composition of what is called the *consideration set*—the brands a customer considers when making a purchase. Generally, the more consideration sets a product is in, the greater the sales that will result. Survey data, including focus groups, are necessary for this metric, although researchers have tried to estimate the set from scanner data. For expensive industrial products, advertising rarely predicts immediate sales but does produce *leads* or inquiries that are followed up by a sales call.

Sales Promotion. Sales promotion metrics include incremental sales, trial, repeat, and ROI. Typically these are estimated using syndicated data sources, but they can also be measured using surveys and internal analyses.

An important distinction can be made between the short- and long-term effects of promotions. While promotions normally generate short-term "bumps" in sales, they can also have negative and long-term effects (Mela, Gupta, and Lehmann 1997) which can be determined with statistical analysis of either syndicated or internal data.

Distribution. Channel metrics include number of distributors, sales, and costs of the distribution structure. For products sold through retail channels, percentage of all commodity volume (ACV) is often monitored. Specific in-store metrics such as the number of shelf facings and shelf height as well as sales per store are also used.

Price. Price metrics include sales and elasticity. Product managers are also interested in price relative to competitors. Particularly for industrial products, the average percentage of list price obtained (or alternatively the percent sold on deal) offers a good measure of the effectiveness of the brand, selling efforts, and other marketing programs. Low percentages indicate that steep discounts are often given to win business.

Salesforce. Productivity (sales revenue per employee) is a standard measure. It is also common to track accounts won and lost and derive statistics for their trends. Measuring salesforce output against goals or quotas is usually part of the compensation program. Finally, it is becoming more common to measure and compensate the salesforce based on customer satisfaction measures.

Customer Service. All products, both physical and services, have important customer service components. Customer service can be the attempted resolution of any customer problem ranging from repair to product usage questions. Some key measures are performance based, such as the average service time, the percentage of problems solved on the first attempt, and service costs. Unsurprisingly, an important customer-based measure is the perceived quality of the service provided by the company.

Web Metrics The Internet has generated its own set of metrics (see Table 5). Sales volume is an obvious metric. Similarly, "hits" or visits and repeat visits are measured. Besides internal measures, companies like Mediametrix and Nielsen's NetRatings supply industry data on site visits. Additionally, site sponsors are interested in the site's "stickiness," how long a visitor stays at a site, and the number of pageviews, how many pages within a site a potential customer visits.

Table 5
Web Metrics and Source of Information

Metric	**Source of Information**
Sales	Internal
Hits/visits/page views	Syndicated, internal
Repeat visits	Syndicated, internal
"Stickiness"	
Conversion rates	Internal
Revenue/customer	Internal
Profit/customer	Internal
Customer acquisition cost	Internal
% revenue from old customers	Internal
Abandoned shopping carts	Internal
Digital/total sales	Internal

With the severe slump in Internet company stocks in 2000, potential investors and analysts began paying more attention to a site's profitability. Therefore, many of the metrics in Table 5 give a "bottom-line" perspective on the website. A key notion is the site's *conversion rate*, the percentage of visitors who are "converted" into buyers. As many as two-thirds of all Web shoppers put items in their virtual shopping cart but never check out. In addition, for the numerous companies that offer online and off-line opportunities to shop, the ratio of digital to total sales is a useful metric.

Industry-Unique Metrics The unique characteristics of some markets may call for correspondingly unique measures. As an example, Table 6 shows some of the consumer and product metrics monitored by the pharmaceuticals, sports, and food industries. In food-related industries, product/brand managers are interested in how free-standing insert (FSI) promotions perform, the "lift," or increased sales, from end-of-aisle displays, and how their marketing strategies affect the interpurchase times of the category and the brand. Pharmaceutical product managers are interested in which doctors are prescribing their drugs, share of prescriptions, and data on diagnoses and new medical procedures. Sports-related marketing managers measure stadium attendance, revenues from licensing logos, and share of market relative to other entertainment products. While recognizing such differences exist, we focus on measures likely to be relevant across a broad spectrum of products.

Table 6
Key Metrics by Industry

Food	**Pharmaceuticals**	**Sports**
Sales	Dollar volume	Attendance
Volume	Doctor surveys	TV ratings
Share	Doctor profiling	Licensing sales
Features	Prescription data	Fan base
Displays	Procedure data	Favorite team
Free-standing inserts (FSIs)	Diagnostic data	Favorite players
Penetration		Fan demographics
Purchase cycle		Share of market
Switching		
Loyalty		
Lift		
Coupons		
Bonus packs		

Summary

We have indicated some of the numerous metrics that can be monitored. The real issue, however, is which of these matter (i.e., relate to financial performance).

Of course, most product managers do not report to the board. Therefore, they concentrate on customer and product market measures for diagnostic purposes and financial measures for evaluating programs and justifying budgets. While monitoring metrics may be less exciting than designing ad copy, it is critical. As many, including Deming, have suggested, if you don't measure it, you won't manage it.

Linking Marketing Actions to Product-Market Performance

Marketing Mix

The link between marketing mix variables and product-market results has been the focus of much of the marketing science literature. Considerable economic modeling work has addressed these issues. However, it has not found wide acceptance in practice because the assumptions are typically quite restrictive, and hence, not realistic (e.g., two competitors, two segments of customers, costs equal to zero, two-period horizon). In general, realistic modeling and mathematical tractability are inconsistent goals. More general models can be addressed with numerical methods including agent-based simulation (Garber et al. 2004; Lusch and Tay 2004). While much of the field seems to consider such approaches intellectually inferior, numerical solutions have much to commend them. Still, for the sake of credibility, empirical results are generally required.

Empirical work on the impact of advertising is widespread, including detailed studies of executional elements (Stewart and Furse 1986). Several meta-analyses (Eastlack and Rao 1986; Assmus, Farley, and Lehmann 1984; Batra et al. 1995; Lodish et al. 1995; Riskey 1997; Sethuraman and Tellis 1991) reveal consistent findings. Spending more money on a mature product with nothing new to say has little short-run impact in terms of sales (elasticity 0–.03), whereas ad spending on a new product or new use of an old product is noticeably more effective (elasticity around .3). This has direct implications for both budget setting and evaluation (i.e., a proposed 50% increase in ad spending for a mature product alone is unlikely to produce a 10% increase in unit sales) and allocation (i.e., generally allocating more to new products with high sales growth than to old products with high sales levels is preferable).

The promotion area has been at least as widely studied (Neslin 2002). Here the evidence generally suggests that promotions have a positive short-run and a negative long-run impact with the total effect positive, at least in the absence of (likely) competitive reactions (e.g., Mela, Gupta, and Lehmann 1997). This is consistent with the noticeable drop in share P&G suffered when it cut promotions and competition failed to follow (Ailawadi, Lehmann, and Neslin 2001).

In addition, several researchers investigate the impact of promotions in the pharmaceutical industry (e.g., Narayanan, Desiraju, and Chintagunta 2004). Once again, the focus of this research has been on sales and not on the impact on perceptions of the brand. Importantly, there is some evidence that if a firm frequently promotes the brand, the customer's perceptions and the brand's equity can be reduced as customers start to infer the brand is of lower quality. Moreover, some customers, having become accustomed to seeing the brand on promotion, only buy it when it is on promotion.

There is less available evidence about the links between channel variables and financial performance. Much of the channels literature focuses on information use and relationship quality (trust, satisfaction) and links these to self-rated performance scales (Moorman, Zaltman, and Deshpandé 1992; Moorman, Deshpandé, and Zaltman 1993). Reibstein and Farris (1995) find the relationship between distribution and market share to be positive, although non-linear, in contrast to the assumption of linearity that is commonplace in most new product forecasting models.

Substantial research also looks at interactions between marketing mix variables. Perhaps most common is the research investigating advertising's impact on prices. Some suggest that advertising allows a firm to charge a higher price by creating greater demand, in essence, shifting the demand curve outward. However, other research shows the opposite, that is, as advertising increases, competition intensifies, and prices to the customer become lower (Cady 1976). Farris and Reibstein (1979) show that there is a tendency for firms to covary advertising and prices and that, in general, firms that raise prices when they increase advertising (or decrease both) tend to be more profitable than firms which take their advertising and prices in opposite directions. Steiner (1973) reconciles these results by observing that when distribution is increased, inter-distributor competition lowers prices to the end consumer, even if the manufacturer's price to the distributor increases.

Taken together, the results are interesting but provide relatively few empirical generalizations and quantitatively estimated contingencies. As a consequence, it is difficult to convince managers that a result such as a 2% increase in sales is likely without a "one-off" special study. Related to this, it is difficult to produce realistic budget and P&L statements a priori. As a consequence, management's attention is diverted from strategic issues to tactical ones such as promotion (Bucklin, Lehmann, and Little 1998), where measurement capabilities are better.

Marketing Capabilities and Strategy

There is substantial work on the impact of brand equity on product market outcomes. Generally, the results show that brand equity reduces sensitivity to price increases and makes advertising more effective as well as directly creating a "revenue premium" for the firm (Ailawadi, Lehmann, and Neslin 2003; Erdem and Sun 2002).

There is a vast literature on metrics related to new products (Hauser, Tellis, and Griffin 2006), much of it focused on development. There has also been considerable effort addressing the pattern of product diffusion, much of it using the Bass (1969) model (Gatignon, Eliashberg, and Robertson 1989; Sultan, Farley, and Lehmann 1990; Golder and Tellis 1997). The Bass model represents the probability of adoption of a new product in the next period, given a person has not yet adopted, as $p + q$ (Past Adoption/Market Potential). Here p represents the tendency to adopt on one's own (innovate) based on company-supplied information, etc., and q represents the tendency to adopt because others have adopted (imitate due to word-of-mouth, etc.). The results suggest that (a) Bass model parameters are 0–.04 for p and .3–.4 for q for consumer durables, (b) there is a lag between introduction and takeoff of several years, and (c) patterns vary by country (Tellis, Stremersch, and Yin 2003).

There has been some investigation on the impact of increasing the firm's product line. Randall, Ulrich, and Reibstein (1998) find that as a firm extends its product line up upward, its brand's equity increases. However, extending the brand upward may make it difficult to sell the product. Volkswagen tried to introduce a luxury end automobile under the Volkswagen name, but found it nearly impossible to do so, and ended up withdrawing the product from the market. By contrast, Toyota decided to introduce the Lexus without associating it under the Toyota name. Conversely, when a firm extends its brand downward, it makes it easier to sell the lower-end offering, but also has a negative impact on the brand's equity. An example of this is Marriott which chose to associate its brand with the lower-end brands in its portfolio.

The impact of new product entry order on sales has also been extensively studied. Most studies find an advantage to early entry (e.g., Kalyanaram, Robinson, and Urban 1995; Szymanski, Troy, and Bharadwaj 1995), although the advantage may be overstated and depends on the ability of the firm to capture the evolving technology and continue to improve its offering (Golder and Tellis 1993). First-mover advantages are not automatic. It is necessary to capitalize on what being first potentially entails: (1) identification with the category, (2) locking up key distribution, (3) controlling critical suppliers, and (4) using the experience with customers to learn how their needs are evolving to generate customer retention. Put differently, being first on average helps but is far from a panacea.

Market Orientation

Numerous studies focus on the link between market orientation and product market results (Kohli and Jaworski 1990; Narver and Slater 1990; Deshpandé, Farley, and Webster 1993). Market orientation has generally been positively linked to market performance (Pelham 1999; Slater and Narver 1994; Pelham and Wilson 1996), although its impact depends on market conditions. More specifically, Dutta, Narasimhan, and Rajiv (1999) demonstrate the importance of marketing capability in high tech markets. Being entrepreneurial and market-oriented are shown to positively impact performance (Matsuno, Mentzer, and Ozsomer 2002). Interestingly, the impact may be more on performance variance than on its level (Capon, Farley, and Hoenig 1990). That is, capabilities such as market orientation (or measures such as satisfaction and customer retention) may have greater impact on the variance than the mean results. If this is the case, then reducing earnings variability can enhance stock price (Srivastava, Fahey, and Christensen 2001).

Kirca, Jayachandran, and Bearden (2005) use meta-analysis to assess the impact of market orientation on intermediate performance as measured by such variables as customer satisfaction and new product performance (and employee attitudes) as well as overall performance (including sales and profits). The relationship is positive, especially for manufacturing (versus service) firms.

Linking Marketing Actions to Financial Performance

This chapter highlights some of the research linking marketing actions directly to financial performance with an emphasis on recent literature. In doing so, we largely overlook the massive literature linking marketing actions to customer-level metrics (which in turn link to financial performance) (a) because all the links in the chain have yet to be established in a quantitative manner which enables an assessment of their profitability versus statistical significance and (b) because of a space (and author energy) constraint.

Marketing Mix

Joshi and Hanssens (2004) link advertising spending to stock performance, echoing the work of Hirschey (1982), Cheng and Chen (1997), and Chauvin and Hirschey (1993). Ho, Keh, and Ong (2005) study the period 1962 to 2001, and conclude that advertising contributes significantly to the stock performance of non-manufacturing (but not manufacturing) firms.

Jose, Nichols, and Stevens (1986) assess the impact of promotion. Ailawadi, Borin, and Farris (1995) demonstrate a link between marketing actions, EVA, and MVA. Other studies address the impact of customer service changes (Nayyar 1995) and event sponsorship (Miyazaki and Morgan 2001) on stock market value, as well as service quality in general (Zeithaml 2000). Erickson and Jacobson (1992) and Graham and Frankenberger (2000) assess the impact of recession on the effectiveness of marketing activities. Recently Pauwels et al. (2004) find that new product introductions, especially in a new market, increase long-term financial performance, but promotions do not.

In the new product area, both Chaney, Devinney, and Winer (1991) and Lane and Jacobson (1995) demonstrate a positive impact of new product announcements on stock price. In fact, the impact of new product announcements and introductions has been studied fairly extensively both inside marketing (Koku, Jagpal, and Viswanath 1997) and outside (Cooper 1984; Eddy and Saunders 1980; Pardue, Higgins, and Biggart 2000). While new product announcements appear to increase stock price, delays in new product introductions decrease it (Hendricks and Singhal 1997), suggesting that only announcements which are accurate have long-run benefits. Radically new products have a positive impact on performance in at least one key industry: pharmaceuticals (Sorescu, Chandy, and Prabhu 2003).

Rust, Zahorik, and Keiningham (1995) assess the financial impact of quality on market value; Hendricks and Singhal (1996) relate quality awards to market value; Ittner and Larcker (1996) study quality initiatives; and Jarrell and Peltzman (1985) show the impact of product recalls. Rust, Moorman, and Dickson (2002) separate the impact of quality into cost reduction and revenue expansion. More generally, one study suggests that ethical behavior may improve financial performance (Cloninger et al. 2000). This raises the question of when "doing well by doing good" is true and when "doing good" requires an objective function broader than profits or stock price.

One interesting approach to studying the impact of marketing spending strategy involves examining the impact of reductions in expenditures to improve current earnings prior to seasoned equity offerings (i.e., the issuing of additional shares of stock). Using this approach, Mizik and Jacobson (2006) note that most firms seem to reduce expenditures and increase income prior to such offerings. Importantly, firms that cut expenditures prior to offerings tend to have lower long-term stock performance.

Strategy and Processes

Linking strategy to performance (Day and Fahey 1988; Doyle 2000a) has a long history, beginning with the PIMS project which originated at GE (Buzzell and Gale 1987). Doukas and Switzer (1992) relate market concentration and stock market valuation, and Rao, Agrawal, and Dahlhoff (2004) find that firms that employ an umbrella (corporate) brand are valued by the stock market more highly than firms with multiple brands, in spite of the potentially greater risk of such a non-diversified strategy. Mizik and Jacobson (2003) examine relative spending on R&D (long-run "value creating") versus advertising and promotion (short-run "value appropriating") activities. They find that while some firms are better off increasing value appropriation, others can improve by specializing in either value creation or value appropriating, depending on their current allocation between the two. Geyskens, Gielens, and Dekimpe (2002) demonstrate a positive impact of adding Internet channels, especially for strong companies and early followers.

Linking Marketing Assets to Financial Performance

This chapter focuses on three key (and related) customer assets that have clear financial impacts: satisfaction, customers, and brands.

Satisfaction

Customer satisfaction has been a central concept in marketing for a long time (e.g., Howard and Sheth 1969; Oliver 1980). Basically, it captures the reaction to a product or service after use (see Zeithaml and Parasuraman 2004). Most current measures are based on the "gap" model (Parasuraman, Zeithaml, and Berry 1988), that is, the difference between expected and actual performance. Evidence suggests that both actual and expected performance also directly impact satisfaction (although in a regression model, only two of the three terms can be included due to collinearity).

Several key questions arise in measuring satisfaction. First, is it "episodic" (i.e., related to a single situation) or cumulative, with the later episodes being both more stable and more closely related to other concepts such as brand equity, quality, and attitude? Second, what are the relevant standards of comparisons; e.g., ideal, "should," or "will" expectations (Boulding et al. 1993) or strategically managed "as if" expectations (Kopalle and Lehmann 2001)? Third, how do comparisons with these standards combine with other considerations such as payoffs (and their equity), procedural justice, etc., to form overall satisfaction? Fourth, do we measure satisfaction for all users, non-users, heavy users, etc., and once measured, do we report it for subgroups, overall, or for some weighted average across groups? Most customer satisfaction measures are taken from the existing customer base with the net result that satisfaction levels will generally increase when dissatisfied customers leave. Most important, is satisfaction an appropriate measure of performance? Many people would argue that satisfaction may not reflect current performance, but is a useful indicator of future performance as it captures the likelihood of customers returning to purchase again (Reichheld 2001).

A tremendous amount of literature focuses on satisfaction as a de facto criterion measure, e.g., the work on salesforce satisfaction and satisfaction with channel partners (Geyskens, Steenkamp, and Kumar 1998). Still, evidence suggests maximizing satisfaction does not necessarily maximize product-market performance (e.g., sales, share, profits) as shown by Ittner and Larcker (1998). They show a non-linear relationship, whereby increasing satisfaction above a certain level no longer has a positive benefit. As a consequence, there may be an optimal level of satisfaction. This makes interpretation of satisfaction scores less straightforward since more is not necessarily better.

Linking Satisfaction to Product-Market Results One clearly established result is that satisfaction is linked to product-market results (Zeithaml and Parasuraman 2004). Satisfaction improves repeat purchase rates and generates favorable word-of-mouth. Using a chain-type model and data from key informants in a commoditized B2B setting, Bowman and Narayandas (2004) demonstrate links between effort (hours spent with the customer) and satisfaction and between satisfaction and profitability. The amount of the increase (e.g., in terms of elasticity), however, is not widely reported and here again empirical generalizations are lacking. Similarly, as in many such correlations, the issue of simultaneity arises. To what extent does satisfaction (dissatisfaction) generate positive (negative) word-of-mouth? How much of satisfaction is dissonance reduction?

One reason for the push for financial metrics is the sometimes weak relationship between mindset measures such as attitude and intention and actual behavior. For example, Seiders et al. (2005) find that the impact of satisfaction is different on repurchase intentions versus actual repeat purchase behavior.

Linking Satisfaction to Financial Performance As suggested earlier, satisfaction is the key mindset metric in terms of predicting retention, and hence customer lifetime value (CLV) and firm value. Importantly, there is evidence that satisfaction relates to firm ROA. Anderson, Fornell, and Lehmann (1994) develop a specific estimate of the impact of a point of satisfaction on ROA and find that a one-point increase in satisfaction (on a 100-point scale) each year over five years generated over a 10% increase in ROA for Swedish firms. Anderson, Fornell, and Rust (1997) compare the impact of satisfaction for goods and services while Hallowell (1996) relates satisfaction directly to profitability. Moreover, Ittner and Larker (1998), Bernhardt, Donthu, and Kennet (2000), and Anderson, Fornell, and Mazvancheryl (2004) demonstrate the link between customer satisfaction at the aggregate level and several measures of shareholder value.

Most recently, Fornell et al. (2006) find that satisfaction not only increases average returns but also lowers risk (variance). Gruca and Rego (2005) also demonstrate that satisfaction (measured by the University of Michigan's American Consumer Satisfaction Index or ACSI) both increases cash flow and decreases its variability. Moreover, the impacts vary substantially across the 23 industries they studied. Interestingly, the link between satisfaction (measured by ACSI) and both short-term profits and the stock market's appraisal of long-run value as measured by Tobin's q is stronger for firms that also focus on cost containment (Mittal et al. 2005). Morgan and Rego (2006b) also link satisfaction measures based on the ACSI to six performance measures: three product-market (sales, margin, share) and three financial (Tobin's q, cash flow, shareholder return) for 80 firms. Interestingly, word-of-mouth seems to drive only share and net promotions have no impact, whereas satisfaction has a major impact on all six performance measures. The key question, then, is not whether satisfaction relates to financial performance, but rather the strength and form (which is logically non-linear) of the relation. Of course, to be useful, we also need to know the impact of marketing actions on satisfaction. While satisfaction is clearly attributable to product and service dimensions, to the degree advertising and sales effort set customer expectations, they too, can have an important impact on satisfaction levels.

Relatively little is known about how other mindset measures can be linked to either product market behavior or financial performance. For example, considerable effort has been expended analyzing brand associations including image and personality. How this translates into sales, profit, etc., is unclear either for specific cases or classes of products in general. Given the current refusal of CEOs to accept "justification by faith" arguments, this poses a relevance problem for marketers working on these fuzzy but potentially critical variables.

Customers

Customer relationship management is one area of marketing where metrics are both widely available and utilized. This work builds heavily on the practices of direct marketing which traditionally kept track of customers on an individual basis and assessed customers in terms of RFM: recency (how recently customers bought something), frequency (how often they bought), and monetary value (how much they bought).

An extensive focus on customers is evident in recent research (e.g., Reinartz and Kumar 2000; Rust, Zeithaml, and Lemon 2000; Blattberg, Getz, and Thomas 2001; Gupta and Lehmann 2005). Importantly, the notion of customers is not restricted to final customers. For example, for franchisers or retail chains, the stores play the role of customers and same-store sales are the equivalent of margin at the individual customer level.

The basic metric in this area is customer lifetime value, which considers the long-run buying behavior of a customer. The principle approach is to treat each customer as an asset that has a probability of ending in each period (i.e., defection) and generates a stream of earnings (net of variable cost) which is then discounted back to the present (Blattberg and Deighton 1996; Berger and Nasr 1998). Cost considerations include both acquisition and retention costs.

At its simplest level, the value of customers is the expected discounted cash flow from customers in the future. It depends on three components: acquisition (rate and cost), retention (rate and cost), and expansion/growth in same customer margin (amount and cost). Obviously, aside from cost, the larger the three components are, the more revenue a firm gets from customers. While all three matter, the leverage a firm gets from increasing retention appears to be the greatest (Gupta and Lehmann 2005).

Of course not all customers are of equal value. Using discounts to acquire customers both attracts customers who have lower reservation prices (i.e., lower utility) for the product and also leads them to infer that the discounted price is the true (fair) one. Lewis (2006) demonstrates that customers acquired via promotions are significantly lower in CLV. For example, a customer acquired with a 35% discount was about half the value of a customer acquired without a discount for an online grocer, but worth 90% for a newspaper.

Fader, Hardie, and Lee (2005) develop a model that formally links RFM to CLV. The model is a continuous analog to the Pareto-NBD (negative binomial distribution) model of Schmittlein, Morrison, and Colombo (1987). Using their model, they assess the value to the firm of a cohort of new customers to the online music site CDNOW.

One implication which results from examining the algebra of CLV as well as other work (Reichheld and Teal 1996) is that retention is key. Retention has more marginal impact on CLV than either acquisition cost or the discount rate. Given this, understanding its antecedents is an important part of developing a value chain. Gustafson, Johnson, and Roos (2005) demonstrate a strong relationship of satisfaction and relationship commitment to retention. Further, they demonstrate the best predictor of churn is prior churn, that is, some customers are inherently more loyal and hence have much larger CLVs. Bolton (1998) also finds an important satisfaction-to-retention link.

Still, maximizing retention probably means "leaving money on the table." Not only does it ignore the fact that some customers are not profitable but it, like satisfaction, is easier to maximize by focusing on a small segment of customers. Also, while retention appears to be the most critical component of CLV, achieving maximum profits from customers requires balancing acquisition and retention efforts (Reinartz, Thomas, and Kumar 2005).

Like all metrics, CLV raises some issues. First, when a customer defects, it may not be forever. However, most simple CLV formulae don't allow for the customer to return. Hogan, Lemon, and Libai (2003) capture this possibility by distinguishing between whether a customer defects to a competitor (from which they may return) or dis-adopts the product category (which means they won't return). Even more fundamental, it is often impossible to say with certainty if a customer has defected for good or merely slowed purchases. While statistical modeling can give some insight here (Schmittlein, Morrison, and Colombo 1987), most CLV formulations are deterministic rather than stochastic. Moreover, most CLV formulas capture only the direct value through purchases. This leaves out both word-of-mouth and network effects, which can be substantial. Also importantly, the data that go into CLV calculations are usually myopic. More specifically, in general databases have information on transactions with only one firm. As a result, they have no sense of either customer potential or their share of market requirements or wallet.

Perhaps most critically, CLV is predicted based on forecasts of customer margin, retention rate, and retention cost. Like most forecasts, this one is based on assumptions and has a notable error associated with it, something which should be explicitly acknowledged (e.g., with a plus or minus range) or explored by presenting alternative scenarios in a sensitivity analysis. Unfortunately, this rarely happens.

The point here is not that CLV is a bad measure. Indeed it has proved quite useful and is related to overall firm value (Gupta, Lehmann, and Stuart 2004). Rather the point is that it, like all metrics, has advantages and disadvantages and provides, to use another metaphor, both highlights and shadows.

Managing customers as assets is now an accepted concept in marketing (Gupta and Lehmann 2005; Bolton, Lemon, and Verhoef 2004; Hogan, Lemon, and Rust 2002). It seems clear customer assets lead to financial performance (Hogan et al. 2002). Customer relationship management (CRM) processes have been shown to improve performance (Ramaswami, Bhargava, and Srivastava 2004; Reinartz, Krafft, and Hoyer 2004). Much of the work on CRM focuses on its impact on intermediate goals such as retention (e.g., Verhoef 2003). Reinartz, Krafft, and Hoyer (2004) assess the impact of CRM processes for relationship initiation (acquisition), maintenance (retention), and termination on performance as measured by ROA. The impact, which depends on having organization support (alignment) and relevant technology, is positive.

Regarding financial consequences, Kim, Mahajan, and Srivastava (1995) use a customer-based method to evaluate cellular communications companies. Hogan, Lemon, and Libai (2003) focus on the value of a customer in terms of their impact on the diffusion process. Gupta and Lehmann (2003) and Gupta, Lehmann, and Stuart (2004) combine diffusion modeling with the CLV concept to value both dot.com and "regular" (e.g., Capital One) companies.

Brands

Brands represent a significant fraction of the intangible, and hence total, value of many firms. This has led to attempts to include brand value on the balance sheets of firms in the U.K. (Kallapur and Kwan 2004). A key issue, therefore, is how to estimate brand value in a standard manner.

Measuring brand value (equity) raises two critical questions. The first question is conceptual: Does brand equity refer to the value of the brand to the customer or the value of the brand to the firm (aggregated across customers)? The value of a brand varies across customers, as not all customers view brands equally. At the individual customer level, it can be measured as the amount extra the customer would be willing to pay for the brand versus a generic equivalent. Yet we often think of the customer-centric value of a brand as reflected in measures such as the awareness, affect, or associations the customer has with the brand. By contrast, firm-level brand value is the consequence of the customers' value that manifests itself in either additional margin or sales. Thus, it is often thought of as incremental revenue accrued by the firm attributable to existence of the brand. Typically, those in the marketing function take the customer-centric view while those higher in the organization or outside marketing take the firm view (Ambler and Barwise 1998).

The second question is whether brand equity can be captured by a single measure. Obviously, for diagnostic purposes, multiple measures are helpful. For example, the sales and price premiums for a brand are components of a variance analysis of the revenue premium and capture different aspects of brand equity at the product-market level. Similarly, awareness, associations, and satisfaction capture different aspects of what consumers think of products. Further, the various components are not necessarily highly correlated, meaning they may not pass the standard tests for undimensionality of a construct. As a consequence, many in marketing argue that no single measure adequately captures the construct. On the other hand, many outside marketing (and some inside it as well) find the discussion of nuances convoluted and not very helpful. They want a single measure because, for example, they have to decide how much to pay to acquire a brand.

As a consequence, brand metrics vary widely (see Table 7). Some are conceptually incomplete but still informative. For example, at the firm level, share contains the effect of other elements of the mix (e.g., price) and competition which need to be removed before brand equity can be assessed. An alternative brand metric, the price premium, is a result of a strategic decision about whether to take the benefits of the brand's equity in volume versus margin. In the metrics value chain, nuanced (multiple) customer-level measures occur at the beginning of the chain whereas firm-level financial market measures represent the end of the chain. In other words, the various measures are causally, if imprecisely, related. Unfortunately, there has been little research into what a firm

Table 7
Perspectives on Brand Equity

Customer-Level Metrics (Value to Customer)	**Firm-Level Metrics (Value to Firm)**
Mindset	Product Market
Awareness	Stocking level (ACV)
Associations	Price premium
Attitude	Sales premium
Attachment (loyalty)	Revenue premium
Activity	Brand constant in a logit model
Behavior	Financial Market
Purchases revenue	Tobin's q
Share of wallet	MVA
Activity	Value in mergers and acquisitions
Financial	Stock price
CLV	Market capitalization

needs to spend in order to either create or maintain brand equity. Similarly, we know very little about how quickly a brand's equity erodes. Both of these are vital for determining the value of marketing spending.

Table 8
Sources of Business Margin by Brand and Customer

	Brand A		Brand B		Total
Customer 1 2	Product 1 a b	Product 2 a b	Product 3 a b	Product 4 a b	a + b values (value of customer)
– – –					
N					
Total a + b Total b	A1 B1 B1	A2 B2 B2	A3 B3 B3	A4 B4 B4	Total net revenue Total brand value

a = Attribute-driven revenue (economic and functional benefits)
b = Brand-driven revenue (extra due to brand)
Note: For each brand there is some revenue driven by the attributes of the brands (A1, A2, A3, A4) and there is some additional revenue driven by the brand name itself (B1, B2, B3, B4). This is true for each product carrying the brand's name and differs by individual.

It is also useful to recognize the relation between brand equity and customer equity. Essentially the value of a customer is the sum across all products a customer purchases. Thus, total customers' lifetime value generally exceeds product-market-level brand equity (see Table 8).

The value of brands is addressed in several studies. Brand quality (Aaker and Jacobson 1994) and attitude (Aaker and Jacobson 2001) both relate to stock value. Interestingly, work in accounting finds similar results (Barth et al. 1998; Amir and Lev 1996). Within marketing, Simon and Sullivan (1993) generate a way to deduce the value of a brand by removing the value of fixed assets and using instrumental variables (advertising and order of entry) to capture the value of marketing. The value of brands ranges from close to zero for commodities (e.g., chemical) to 30–50% of the value of tangibles for consumer goods. Mahajan, Rao, and Srivastava (1994) provide a method for assessing the value of a brand in acquisitions. Brand value is clearly linked to stock value (Kerin and Sethuraman 1998) and, not surprisingly, changing a brand name has a financial impact (Horsky and Swyngedouw 1987). The link of brands to shareholder value is further demonstrated by Madden, Fehle, and Fournier (2006).

For firms that have multiple brands, an obvious question is how best to position them in terms of quality, price, and similarity to each other. Based on data for 149 Fortune 500 companies from 1994 to 2000 that are included in the American Consumer Satisfaction Index, Morgan and Rego (2006b) find different strategies produce different results. Focusing on quality and targeting brands to different segments enhances loyalty, whereas share goals require a large number of and lower quality brands. Most important, competitors with large portfolios and high-quality products have better financial performance as measured by Tobin's q.

Methodological Approaches and Issues

Cross-sectional versus Time-Series Data

Few impacts are truly instantaneous. Hence, in principle all analysis should be time-series in nature. However, time-series data are often difficult to assemble. Further, the choice of what periodicity to employ (daily, monthly, yearly) impacts the results. Thus, a problem exists concerning the appropriate level of data aggregation and the consequences of using sub-optimal ones.

Time-series data allow for testing the impact of marketing over time. They also raise the issue of whether an effect lasts one period, a few periods (a.k.a. the "dust-settling" period), or is permanent (Dekimpe and Hanssens 2004). Research suggests that tactics such as promotion and advertising have no long-run (permanent) impact in the vast majority of cases (Dekimpe and Hanssens 1999).

The choice of cross-sectional versus time-series data (as well as the level of aggregation) also impacts the results. For example, Rindfleisch et al. (2004) demonstrate that using cross-sectional versus time-series data sometimes produces noticeably different results.

The Impact of Competition

Competition is often ignored in assessing the impact of marketing. One reason is that the complexity of competitive behavior drives many researchers to use the "reduced form" model of "we do X and the result is Y" without trying to capture the competitive reaction. Another reason for using "myopic" models is data availability. This is a particular concern in the customer relationship management area: data typically contain detailed information about customers' behavior—but with respect to only one firm. What business customers do with other competitors is usually not part of the database.

That competition reaction occurs is well established; less well known is *when* and *how* competitors react. Some work suggests that competitors react immediately to a firm's actions regardless of the impact (Debruyne and Reibstein 2005). Other work suggests that firms take a "wait and see" stance and only react either if their own performance is affected or if the competition firm's actions reap positive results. The timing and strength of competitive reaction is important in assessing the overall impact of any marketing action.

Recently, considerable effort has gone into adopting the new industrial organization approach (NEIO) to modeling competition (Chintagunta, Kadiyali, and Vilcassim 2004). An open question is whether incomplete specification of such a model produces better estimates than a myopic model that ignores competition.

Subjective versus Objective Performance Measures

A potentially important but little-considered issue is the distinction between objective and subjective measures. Objective measures such as sales or profits are inherently absolute and, hence, comparable across as well as within industries. Subjective measures are often employed for reasons of convenience and availability. They can be simple estimates of the "true" objective measure (e.g., "what were sales last year?") which add noise (error) to the analysis and may or may not be biased (i.e., consistently under- or over-estimate performance). Alternatively, as is frequently the case, performance measures can be truly subjective (e.g., "How well did your company perform in terms of new product development?"). Here the implicit standard of comparison used (e.g., last year's level, industry average, best in class) will impact results.

One of the earliest projects to systematically relate marketing to performance, the PIMS project, relies heavily on relative, subjective measures (i.e. "relative to competition, was your _____ well above average, above average, . . . ?"). This of course raises issues of comparability in cross-industry studies: what is a good subjective assessment in one industry may be poor in another.

One study that addresses the issue of subjective versus objective measures is Ailawadi, Dant, and Grewal (2004). Using concepts such as positivity bias, cognitive consistency, and self-serving attributions, they anticipated a possible mismatch between subjective and objective measures. They examine five years of data on sales agents' performance collected by both surveys of the agents and archival data. The resulting correlations between subjective and objective measures are in the range of .3 and the subjective responses are systematically related to a number of factors such as experience.

Since the use of subjective measures is widespread in work on channel partnerships and market orientation as well, future research is needed to calibrate the effect of using subjective measures on links in the model. While it is unlikely that results using subjective measures are solely due to response style and method effects, it is likely that subjective data lead to overstating the strength of some links in the value chain.

Statistical Methods

Persistence Modeling   One key problem, as discussed above, is that it is difficult to assess impacts over time. For example, promotion may have a positive short-run but a negative long-run impact (Mela, Gupta, and Lehmann 1997). One approach for separating immediate, intermediate ("dust-settling"), and long-run impacts is persistence modeling (Dekimpe and Hanssens 2004), a form of time-series modeling. For the most part, these models have been used to assess the impact of marketing actions (primarily promotion and advertising) on product-market performance, in particular sales. Interestingly, one study (Villanueva, Yoo, and Hanssens 2003) demonstrates that CLV is related to the channel by which customers are acquired.

Event Studies   When a marketing activity is a discrete event significant enough to have a measurable impact on stock value (or more precisely on stock returns), then a direct approach is appropriate. If the impact is immediate and fairly large, then an event study approach is relevant (see Srinivasan and Bharadwaj 2004 for a concise explanation). The basic idea is that the stock price captures expected future revenue and change in the stock price reflects anticipated changes in future revenue, in effect instantaneously capturing the value of a change in marketing actions. The basic approach is to compare stock price adjusted for general stock market conditions before and after the event (e.g., a new product introduction) occurs. In practice, issues arise with respect to establishing when the event occurred (or if it occurred gradually), the length of the event "window"—how long a period you use to measure the impact—and how much the pre-event period is impacted by information about the forthcoming event.

Encouragingly, event studies based on daily prices demonstrate significant impact to some marketing actions. Company name changes (Horsky and Swyngedouw 1987) and celebrity endorsements (Agrawal and Kamakura 1995) generally impact stock price positively as do new product announcements (Chaney, Devinney, and Winer 1991; Lane and Jacobson 1995). Similarly, discrete partner-related activities such as joint ventures and Internet channel additions appear to generate positive movements in stock price (Houston and Johnson 2000; Geyskens, Gielens, and Dekimpe 2002).

Stock Market Modeling Many impacts are less dramatic than those which can be captured by event analysis and occur gradually over time. While this can be handled with long event windows, such windows inevitably are confounded with numerous other changes in the firm, competition, etc. As a consequence, an econometric (regression-like) procedure known as stock return modeling is applicable (Mizik and Jacobson 2004). Basically this approach models stock returns as a function of the expected returns, accounting performance (earnings, etc.), and marketing strategy (e.g., market orientation) across a set of firms. The effect of marketing strategy that results from analyzing pooled cross-section, time-series databases have shown significant positive returns to perceived quality (Aaker and Jacobson 1994) and *Financial World*'s brand equity measure and change in brand attitude for high-tech firms (Aaker and Jacobson 2001). Interestingly, the impact of a firm's relative emphases on R&D versus marketing depends on industry and firm factors (Mizik and Jacobson 2003).

Meta-analysis   As previously mentioned, meta-analysis has the potential to facilitate estimating links in the metrics value chain. Links in the chain are likely to differ by situation and be impacted by modeling, data, and estimation method. This means that the search for a single constant estimate of each link is likely to be fruitless. On the other hand, there may well be a central tendency and key contingencies that account for systematic differences in the links. Hence by looking across a broad array of situations, empirical generalizations may be uncovered.

Conceptually, this is the basic problem that meta-analysis is designed to address (Farley, Lehmann, and Sawyer 1995; Farley et al. 2004). Whether within study (which requires a massive data collection effort by a single team of researchers) or, as is the typical case, cross-study (e.g., based on published research), meta-analysis can establish both the mean size of a link (e.g., the impact of satisfaction on share) and an estimate of how much the link varies under different circumstances (i.e., in monopoly versus competitive situations).

Of course any meta-analysis also has problems. These include the representativeness of the available studies and confounding of possible determinants of differences in the results due to the unplanned natural experiment that produced available results. In fact, confounding is common due to a cascade effect in published studies (e.g., a prevalence of studies on consumer goods in the U.S. using scanner data).

Other Approaches   Time-series analysis and meta-analysis are not the only ways to assess links in the chain. For example, if a binary measure such as firm survival or new product success is the focus, hazard modeling approaches can be employed. Basically, these approaches link survival to a number of possible determinants through a hazard function which is similar to a regression model. These approaches are often used to assess customer retention, product adoption, and sales takeoff (Bowman 2004). Another approach is so-called structural modeling (Chintagunta, Kadiyali, and Vilcassim 2004) which assesses product-market impacts explicitly taking into account the appropriate (optimal) behavior of competitors.

Comprehensive Testing

There are two approaches to comprehensively examining the metrics value chain. The first is to collect data on all the measures for a sample of companies and analyze results in a multiple equation model. While this is clearly desirable, it involves a level of data collection that is at best difficult. A starting point would be to take one firm, collect the measures in the metrics value chain, and estimate the relationships among them.

The second is to take estimates of different links from different studies as is sometimes done in meta-analyses in the management area. This involves some important technical issues; for example, correlation matrices assembled this way may not be positively definite (which makes parameter estimates unreliable at best) and the correlations may be impacted by peculiar conditions of the study from which they are taken. Still, it may provide a useful starting point for producing the kind of general model that will resonate in boardrooms. In fact, meta-analysis appears to be the best way to establish typical measures of the strength of the various links in the chain as well as to uncover important systematic variance in the strength. It also provides a prior which can improve the estimates of links in a particular situation. Thus, meta-analysis seems to be the tool of choice for generating general knowledge about links in the chain.

Estimating Effects and Action Optimization

An obvious question is how to optimize marketing activities and budgets. One approach is to develop reduced-form models that link firm actions directly to stock price. Unfortunately, many marketing actions are not likely to produce a measurable change in the stock price (e.g., a promotion for one of P&G's many brands). Even if the link is clear, the reduced-form model provides little diagnostic information as to the process or timeline by which results emerge (e.g., do promotions increase acquisitions or retention and what is the time path of the results).

Another approach is to break the problem down into components, separately estimating direct links in the metric value chain. The total effect would then be estimated by multiplying through the links in the chain (as in path analysis). Unfortunately, the variance of a product is the product of the variances, each of which is large at this state of knowledge development. The result is high uncertainty about impacts.

The problem is equally severe for analytical analysis. In addition to uncertainty over links and the impact of the assumptions made, there is the problem of non-linearity. If all the links are linear, then the optimal level of an action tends to be zero or infinity. On the other hand, non-linear models are more difficult to estimate and produce even greater variance in estimates.

Timing of Effects

An important decision that impacts marketing is the accounting practice of expensing marketing expenditures. This results in an assessment of marketing's impact in the period in which the expenditure occurs. Yet, it is well known that much of marketing has (a) a cumulative impact and (b) a residual impact, that is, its impact may be enduring. For example, to acquire a customer may require repeated ads or visits such that only after a threshold is met does the client become a customer (the cumulative impact). Once they become a customer, they may continue to buy from the firm for years to come, hence the CLV calculation (the enduring impact). Consequently, evaluating the impact of marketing only in its current period may lead to underestimating its true value. To complicate matters further, not all marketing expenditures have an impact in the same periodicity, and the elements of the metrics value chain may be measured in different time intervals.

Conclusions

Measures Used in Practice

Several studies investigate the measures used to assess general marketing performance (Bonoma and Clark 1988; Clark 1999; Ambler and Kokkinaki 1997; Ambler 2003). Many others focus on more specific aspects such as salesforce performance (e.g., Cravens et al. 1993). One of the most comprehensive studies involves a survey of both marketing and finance executives in the U.K. (Ambler, Kokkinaki, and Puntoni 2002). Unsurprisingly financial metrics such as profit and margin were the most frequently measured and most important, followed by sales and share.

One question is whether metrics are unique in terms of industry or country. Ambler and Riley (2000) assess metrics use in the U.K. and Spain. Barwise and Farley (2003) examine metrics reported to the board (see Table 9). Share was the most frequently reported metric in Europe (Germany, U.K., France) while quality was in the U.S. and Japan. Overall, share was the most widely reported (79%) followed by quality, (77%), loyalty/retention (64%), customer or segment profitability (64%), relative price (63%), and either actual or potential customer or segment lifetime value (40%). Farley, Hoenig, and Lehmann (2005) study business units in Vietnam. Reported metric use was generally high, with the exception of CLV measures. Among member companies of the Marketing Science Institute, Winer (2000) finds many metrics were industry based such as scanner-based sales and share data for food companies, sales (scripts) by brand by doctor for pharmaceuticals, and attendance and licensing fees for sports teams.

Toward a Common Metric Chain

Obviously, specific actions, situations, and strategies require specific metrics. For example, for a new product it is helpful to have customer

Table 9
Percent of Firms Reporting Metric to Board

Marketing Metric	U.S. (N = 224)	Japan (N = 117)	Germany (N = 120)	U.K. (N = 120)	France (N = 116)	Overall
Market share	73	57	97	80	90	79
Perceived product/service quality	77	68	84	71	75	77
Customer loyalty/retention	67	56	69	58	65	64
Customer/segment profitability	73	40	74	65	59	64
Relative price	65	48	84	53	63	63
Actual/potential customer/segment lifetime value	32	35	51	32	58	40
Average	64	51	77	60	68	

Source: Barwise and Farley (2003)

ratings of comparisons with substitutes, actual switching patterns, customer ratings of relative advantage, compatibility and risk, etc. Still, considering marketing as a whole, it would be useful to have a common metric chain which could be used in multiple situations to improve communication with those outside marketing and to force a disciplined look at marketing productivity. In addition, this would create a consistent set of variables against which to assess the impact of various marketing programs and processes. This in turn would help create a database for establishing a set of empirical generalizations of the strength of the links, as well as how the impacts of programs flow from the customer (final and trade) level through product-market results to financial performance and processes, via meta-analysis. To that end, the value chain model presents a simplified set of measures which flow from customer (final and trade) level through product-market results to financial performance. Because for many firms the critical immediate customer is the channel (consider P&G and Wal-Mart), a few channel-level metrics are also included.

Of course not all these measures need be used in all situations. For example, considerable commercial work exists in measuring brand equity (e.g., Y & R's Brand Asset Valuator—BAV, Millward-Brown's Brand Z, and Research International Equity Engine). While these represent multiple constructs, they are highly correlated due to respondent fatigue, halo effects, and the tendency of many variables to vary at the category level more than at the brand level. As a consequence, measures of (1) awareness (presence, knowledge), (2) key associations, (3) overall attitude (preference, liking), (4) attachment (loyalty), and (5) activity (e.g., how frequently they discuss the product) should suffice and largely form a hierarchy. At the product market level, unit sales and price are key as is the revenue premium versus generic sales which serves as a manifest measure of that period's value of the brand (brand equity).

Open Issues

In introducing the 2005 special section of the *Journal of Marketing*, Boulding et al. (2005) laid out several questions and directions for future research:

1. Are metrics global, pan-industry?
2. Does one size fit all firm types?
3. Missing links
    a. Empirical generalizations
    b. A new PIMS?

Table 10 describes areas where we have specific estimates of links as well as some areas where more knowledge is needed.

Growth: The Ultimate Metric?

Most discussions of metrics sooner or later come around to the issue of whether metrics are (and should be) backward looking (assess past and current position) or forward looking (i.e., project future changes). In fact, most objective metrics are, when expressed as levels, backward looking. Whether it be with awareness or attitude levels in a sample or actual sales or share, marketing databases are largely populated by historical measures. Even the celebrated information systems of Wal-Mart,

Table 10
Current State of Knowledge

Areas where current knowledge provides specific estimates of links:
Advertising spending to sales
Price to sales
The pattern of new product diffusion (sales)
Promotion to short-run sales
Satisfaction to financial results

Links where more knowledge is needed:
Company action to competitive action and vice versa
Product-market results to financial performance
Satisfaction to consumer behavior (repeat rates)
The impact of environmental influences

---

which essentially keep continuous track of sales and inventory, are historical—albeit with a very short lag.

On the other hand, the analyses done on historical data are often employed to predict the future. Models linking the marketing mix elements to sales or share are used to make "what if" assessments and adjust the mix accordingly, and patterns in the historical measures are used to project into the future.

The push for metrics and marketing productivity is appropriate. Nonetheless, ask a manager whether the fascination with marketing metrics would be so great if a business's net revenue were growing at a substantial rate (e.g., 25% per year) and the answer would likely be no. In other words, growth is essentially the "ultimate" metric.

The importance of growth for a publicly traded company is fairly obvious. According to the efficient market hypothesis (which may or may not be accurate in the short run but which tends to be accurate in the long run), the value of a stock is the discounted cash flow (profit) of future earnings. Thus the market capitalization of a firm is

$$\text{Market Cap} = (\text{Current Earnings})\,(P/E)$$

Illegal (and unwise) manipulations aside, current earnings are fixed. Therefore, the price/earnings (*P/E*) ratio represents a forward-looking assessment of the value of a firm.

Using the analogy to the CLV formula discussed earlier, this means for a firm with a constant margin growth rate (and a retention rate of 1) and a 10% discount rate, the *P/E* ratio of a firm should be, ceteris paribus, $1/(i-g)$, assuming g is less than i. Thus for a 10% cost of capital, *P/E* will be 10 for constant earnings (i.e., a perpetuity). For a positive 3% growth rate, the *P/E* rises to over 14 and for 5% to 20. On the other hand, a negative 5% growth rate drives the *P/E* down to under 7. It is no surprise, therefore, that CEOs and CFOs worry about growth and the *P/E* ratio which represents a forecast of future earnings.

$$\hat{g} = \frac{i(P/E) - 1}{P/E}$$

Summary

While the push for metrics has substantial backing and currency, it also has detractors. We make no pretense about resolving this debate. Rather, we side with the argument that measurement is generally good and, recognizing the stress on metrics driven by CEOs and financial markets, discuss briefly what metrics might be considered and how they are linked together and, importantly, to financial performance and firm value.

We have not addressed some key organizational metrics which influence employee behavior and hence customers. These include, among others, market orientation and employee satisfaction. Instead, we have concentrated on the metrics most relevant to marketers or those they report to.

Conceptually, it is useful to think of a metrics value chain as the key tool for monitoring marketing actions. Practically, however, it is difficult to estimate all the links in such a chain in a given situation. This suggests the use of information in other situations (i.e., meta-analysis) to help estimate the links in a particular case. It also suggests that some type of simulation be done to capture variance in outcomes. For example, by generating pessimistic (assuming the low end of the range for the parameters on each link), best guess, and optimistic scenarios, a better sense of the impact of various marketing actions can be generated. In the absence of the ability to assess all the links for a specific firm, the best option would be to estimate the links that are feasible, use the results from meta-analysis for others, and then to use judgment to complete the rest of the metrics value chain. Making explicit the judgments on these links makes the assumptions visible to others, subject to being challenged and, when they pass scrutiny, available for use in other situations.

Where are we in terms of developing a reasonable consensus on the metrics value chain? In terms of what the elements of the chain and the links are, there is reasonable convergence around something close to the value chain in Figure 1, although no single chain has the status of, say, the capital asset pricing model (CAPM) in finance. If something like the value chain becomes widely accepted, several benefits will emerge. First, marketing would have a common paradigm to explain itself to those both within and outside the field. Second, the role of different people becomes clear. Psychologically oriented researchers working early in the chain and financially oriented ones working on links to (stock) market performance would complement each other rather than compete. Finally, we can begin to collect information on the links in the chain across situations to establish general patterns. Such patterns facilitate disciplined thinking and budgeting (i.e., if a budget implies strength of effects 10 times the top of the range of previous results, some serious questioning of the assumptions is called for).

When taken together, the studies mentioned here (and others unmentioned) constitute a serious and impressive body of work. What do they show? Several important findings emerge:

- Retention drives CLV.
- CLV drives stock value.
- Satisfaction drives retention (and therefore CLV) and stock value.
- New products enhance stock value.

Where are we in terms of generating empirical generalizations about the numerical size of the various links? Sadly, we are not very far along. While some links have a history of study which already have or could be turned into specific parameter estimates for the strength of the links, many others do not (see Table 10). Also, importantly, most of the estimates available are based on linking two of the elements only, the equivalent of simple correlations. Such under-specification leads to potential problems and biases in the results. Thus, in addition to more studies linking particular elements in the chain, comprehensive studies are needed which estimate the entire chain in a multi-equation model framework. We hope our brief discussion of the topic, along with the list of references and MSI working papers included here, will provide a start in that direction.

References

Aaker, David A., and Robert Jacobson (1994), "The Financial Information Content of Perceived Quality." *Journal of Marketing* 58 (May), 191–201.

Aaker, David A., and Robert Jacobson (2001), "The Value Relevance of Brand Attitude in High-Technology Markets." *Journal of Marketing Research* 38 (November), 485–93.

Agrawal, Jagdish, and Wagner A. Kamakura (1995), "The Economic Worth of Celebrity Endorsers: An Event Study Analysis." *Journal of Marketing* 59 (July), 56–62.

Ailawadi, Kusum, Norm Borin, and Paul Farris (1995), "Market Power and Performance: A Cross-Industry Analysis of Manufacturers and Retailers." *Journal of Retailing* 71 (3), 211–48.

Ailawadi, Kusum, Rajiv P. Dant, and Dhruv Grewal (2004), "The Difference Between Perceptual and Objective Performance Measures: An Empirical Analysis." Cambridge, Mass.: Marketing Science Institute, Report No. 04-103.

Ailawadi, Kusum L., Donald R. Lehmann, and Scott A. Neslin (2001), "Market Response to a Major Policy Change in the Marketing Mix: Learning from Procter & Gamble's Value Pricing Strategy." *Journal of Marketing* 65 (January), 44–61.

Ailawadi, Kusum L., Donald R. Lehmann, and Scott A. Neslin (2003), "Revenue Premium as an Outcome Measure of Brand Equity." *Journal of Marketing* 67 (October), 1–17.

Ambler, Tim (2003), *Marketing and the Bottom Line: The New Metrics of Corporate Wealth*, 2nd ed. London, U.K.: Financial Times/Prentice Hall, Pearson Education.

Ambler, Tim, and Patrick Barwise (1998), "The Trouble with Brand Valuation." *Journal of Brand Management* 5 (May), 367–77.

Ambler, Tim, and Flora Kokkinaki (1997), "Measures of Marketing Success." *Journal of Marketing Management* 13 (7), 665–78.

Ambler, Tim, Flora Kokkinaki, and S. Puntoni (2002), "Assessing Market Performance: The Current State of Metrics." London, U.K.: London Business School, Centre for Marketing, Working Paper No. 01–903.

Ambler, Tim, and Debra Riley (2000), "Marketing Metrics: A Review of Performance Measures in Use in the U.K. and Spain." Cambridge, Mass.: Marketing Science Institute, Report No. 00–500.

Amir, Eli, and Baruch Lev (1996), "Value Relevance of Non-Financial Information: The Wireless Communication Industry." *Journal of Accounting and Economics* 22 (1–3), 13–20.

Anderson, Eugene W., Claes Fornell, and Donald R. Lehmann (1994), "Customer Satisfaction, Market Share, and Profitability: Findings from Sweden." *Journal of Marketing* 58 (July), 53–66.

Anderson, Eugene W., Claes Fornell, and Sanal K. Mazvancheryl (2004), "Customer Satisfaction and Shareholder Value." *Journal of Marketing* 68 (October), 172–85.

Anderson, Eugene W., Claes Fornell, and Roland Rust (1997), "Customer Satisfaction, Productivity, and Profitability: Differences Between Goods and Services." *Marketing Science* 16 (2), 129–45.

Assmus, Gert, John U. Farley, and Donald R. Lehmann (1984), "How Advertising Affects Sales: Meta-Analysis of Econometric Results." *Journal of Marketing Research* 21(February), 65–74.

Barth, M.E., M. Clement, G. Foster, and R. Kasznik (1998), "Brand Values and Capital Market Valuation." *Review of Accounting Studies* 3 (1–2), 41–68.

Barwise, Patrick, and John U. Farley (2003), "Which Marketing Metrics Are Used and Where?" *Marketing Reports* 2, 105–7.

Bass, Frank M. (1969), "A New Product Growth Model for Consumer Durables." *Management Science* 15 (January), 215–27.

Batra, Rajeev, Donald R. Lehmann, Joanne Burke, and Jae Pae (1995), "When Does Advertising Have an Impact? A Study of Tracking Data." *Journal of Advertising Research* 35 (September–October), 19–32.

Berger, Paul D., and Nada I. Nasr (1998), "Customer Lifetime Value: Marketing Models and Applications." *Journal of Interactive Marketing* 12 (1), 17–30.

Bernhardt, Kenneth, Naveen Donthu, and Pamela Kennet (2000), "A Longitudinal Analysis of Satisfaction and Profitability." *Journal of Business Research* 47 (2), 161–71.

Bhattacharya, C. B., and Leonard M. Lodish (1999), "Brand Health: Basic Concepts and a Store Scanner Data Application." Philadelphia, Penn.: University of Pennsylvania, The Wharton School, Marketing Department, Working Paper No. 99–022.

Blattberg, Robert, and John Deighton (1996), "Manage Marketing by the Customer Equity Test." *Harvard Business Review* 75 (4), 136–44.

Blattberg, Robert, Gary Getz, and Jacquelyn S. Thomas (2001), *Customer Equity: Building and Managing Relationships as Valuable Assets*. Boston, Mass.: Harvard Business School Press.

Bolton, Ruth N. (1998), "A Dynamic Model of the Duration of the Customer's Relationship with a Continuous Service Provider: The Role of Satisfaction." *Marketing Science* 17 (1), 45–65.

Bolton, Ruth N., Katherine N. Lemon, and Peter Verhoef (2004), "The Theoretical Underpinnings of Customer Asset Management: A Framework and Propositions for Future Research." *Journal of the Academy of Marketing Science* 32 (3) (Summer), 271–92.

Bonoma, Thomas V., and Bruce C. Clark (1988), *Marketing Performance Assessment*. Boston, Mass.: Harvard Business School Press.

Boulding, William, Ajay Kalra, Richard Staelin, and Valarie Zeithaml (1993), "A Dynamic Process Model of Service Quality: From Expectations to Behavioral Intentions." *Journal of Marketing Research* 30 (February), 7–27.

Boulding, William, Richard Staelin, Michael Ehret, and Wesley J. Johnston (2005), "A Customer Relationship Management Roadmap: What Is Known, Potential Pitfalls, and Where to Go." *Journal of Marketing* 69 (October), 155–66.

Bowman, Douglas (2004), "Survival Models for Marketing Strategy." In *Assessing Marketing Strategy Performance*, eds. Christine Moorman and Donald R. Lehmann, 115–43. Cambridge, Mass.: Marketing Science Institute.

Bowman, Douglas, and Das Narayandas (2004), "Linking Customer Management Effort to Customer Profitability in Business Markets." *Journal of Marketing Research* 41 (November), 433–47.

Bucklin, Randolph E., Donald R. Lehmann, and John D.C. Little (1998), "From Decision Support to Decision Automation: A 2020 Vision." *Marketing Letters* 9 (August), 235–46.

Buzzell, Robert D., and Bradley T. Gale (1987), *The PIMS Principles: Linking Strategy to Performance*. New York, N.Y.: Free Press.

Cady, John (1976), "Advertising Restrictions and Retail Prices." *Journal of Advertising Research* 16 (5), 27–30.

Capon, Noel, John U. Farley, and Scott Hoenig (1990), "Determinants of Financial Performance: A Meta-Analysis." *Management Science* 36 (October), 1143–59.

Chaney, Paul K., Timothy M. Devinney, and Russell S. Winer (1991), "The Impact of New Product Introductions on the Market Value of Firms." *Journal of Business* 64 (4), 573–610.

Chauvin, Keith W., and Mark Hirschey (1993), "Advertising, R&D Expenditures, and the Market Value of the Firm." *Financial Management* 22 (4), 128–40.

Cheng, C.S. Agnes, and J.P. Charles Chen (1997), "Firm Valuation of Advertising Expense: An Investigation of Scalar Effects." *Managerial Finance* 23 (10), 41–62.

Chintagunta, Pradeep K., Vrinda Kadiyali, and Naufel J. Vilcassim (2004), "Structural Models of Competition: A Marketing Strategy Perspective." In *Assessing Marketing Strategy Performance*, eds. Christine Moorman and Donald R. Lehmann, 95–114. Cambridge, Mass.: Marketing Science Institute.

Clark, Bruce H. (1999), "Marketing Performance Measures: History and Interrelationships." *Journal of Marketing Management* 15 (8) (November), 711–32.

Cloninger, Dale O., Raj Aggarwal, Jonathan Karpoff, Nelson J. Lacey, and Clifford Smith (2000), "Doing Well by Doing Good: Do Financial Markets 'Price' Ethical Behavior?" *Financial Practice and Education* (Fall–Winter), 24–33.

Cooper, Robert G. (1984), "How New Product Strategies Impact on Financial Performance." *Journal of Product Innovation Management* 1 (1), 5–18.

Cravens, David W., Thomas N. Ingram, Raymond W. LaForge, and Clifford E. Young (1993), "Behavior-Based and Outcome-Based Sales Force Control Systems." *Journal of Marketing* 57 (October), 47–59.

Day, George, and Liam Fahey (1988), "Valuing Market Strategies." *Journal of Marketing* 52 (July), 45–57.

Debruyne, Marion, and David Reibstein (2005), "Competitor See, Competitor Do: Incumbent Entry in New Market Niches." *Marketing Science* 24 (1) (Winter), 55–66.

Dekimpe, Marnik, and Dominique Hanssens (1999), "Sustained Spending and Persistent Response: A New Look at Long-Term Marketing Profitability." *Journal of Marketing Research* 36 (November), 1–31.

Dekimpe, Marnik G., and Dominique M. Hanssens (2004), "Persistence Modeling for Assessing Marketing Strategy Performance." In *Assessing Marketing Strategy Performance*, eds. Christine Moorman and Donald R. Lehmann, 69–94. Cambridge, Mass.: Marketing Science Institute.

Deshpandé, Rohit, John U. Farley, and Frederick E. Webster Jr. (1993), "Corporate Culture, Customer Orientation, and Innovativeness in Japanese Firms: A Quadrad Analysis." *Journal of Marketing* 57 (January), 23–37.

Doukas, John, and Lorne Switzer (1992), "The Stock Market's Valuation of R&D Spending and Market Concentration." *Journal of Economics and Business* 44, 95–114.

Doyle, Peter (2000a), *Value-Based Marketing: Marketing Strategies for Corporate Growth and Shareholder Value*. New York, N.Y.: John Wiley & Sons, Ltd.

Doyle, Peter (2000b), "Valuing Marketing's Contribution." *European Management Journal* 18 (3), 232–45.

Dutta, Shantanu, Om Narasimhan, and Surendra Rajiv (1999), "Success in High-Technology Markets: Is Marketing Capability Critical?" *Marketing Science* 18 (4), 547-68.

Eastlack, Joseph O. Jr., and Ambar G. Rao (1986), "Modeling Response to Advertising and Pricing Changes for 'V-8' Cocktail Vegetable Juice." *Marketing Science* 5 (Summer), 245–59.

Eddy, A., and G. Saunders (1980), "New Product Announcements and Stock Prices." *Decision Sciences* 11, 90–97.

Erdem, Tulin, and Baohong Sun (2002), "An Empirical Investigation of the Spillover Effects of Advertising and Sales Promotions in Umbrella Branding." *Journal of Marketing Research* 39 (November), 408–20.

Erickson, Gary, and Robert Jacobson (1992), "Gaining Competitive Advantage Through Discretionary Expenditures: The Returns to R&D and Advertising," *Management Science* 38, 1264–79.

Fader, Peter S., Bruce G.S. Hardie, and Ka Lok Lee (2005), "RFM and CLV: Using Iso-Value Curves for Customer Base Analysis." *Journal of Marketing Research* 42 (November), 415–30.

Farley, John U., Scott Hoenig, and Donald R. Lehmann (2005), "Metrics Use and its Link to Performance in a Transition Economy: The Case of Vietnam." Hanover, N.H.: Dartmouth College, Working Paper.

Farley, John U., Scott Hoenig, Donald R. Lehmann, and David M. Szymanski (2004), "Assessing the Impact of Marketing Strategy Using Meta-Analysis." In *Assessing Marketing Strategy Performance*, eds. Christine Moorman and Donald R. Lehmann, 145–64. Cambridge, Mass.: Marketing Science Institute.

Farley, John U., Donald R. Lehmann, and Alan Sawyer (1995), "Empirical Marketing Generalization Using Meta-Analysis." *Marketing Science* 14 (3, part 2), G36–46.

Farris, Paul W., Neil T. Bendle, Phillip E. Pfeifer, and David Reibstein (2006), *Marketing Metrics: 50+ Metrics Every Executive Should Master*. Upper Saddle River, N.J: Wharton School Publishing.

Farris, Paul W., and Michael J. Moore, eds. (2004), *The Profit Impact of Marketing Strategy Project: Retrospect and Prospects.* Cambridge, U.K.: Cambridge University Press.

Farris, Paul W., and David Reibstein (1979), "How Prices, Ad Expenditures, and Profits Are Linked." *Harvard Business Review* 57 (November/December), 173–84.

Fornell, Claes, Sunil Mithas, Forrest Morgeson, and M.S. Krishnan (2006), "Customer Satisfaction and Stock Prices: High Returns, Low Risk." *Journal of Marketing* 70 (January), 3–14.

Garber, Tal, Jacob Goldenberg, Barak Libai, and Eitan Muller (2004), "From Density to Destiny: Using Spatial Dimension of Sales Data for Early Prediction of New Product Success." *Marketing Science* 23 (3), 419–28.

Gatignon, Hubert, Jehoshua Eliashberg, and Thomas S. Robertson (1989), "Modeling Multinational Diffusion Patterns: An Efficient Methodology." *Marketing Science* 8 (3), 231–47.

Geyskens, Inge, Katrijn Gielens, and Marnik G. Dekimpe (2002), "The Market Valuation of Internet Channel Additions." *Journal of Marketing* 66 (April), 102–19.

Geyskens, Inge, Jan-Benedict E.M. Steenkamp, and Nirmalya Kumar (1998), "Generalizations about Trust in Marketing Channel Relationships Using Meta-Analysis." *International Journal of Research in Marketing* 15 (3), 223–48.

Golder, Peter N., and Gerard J. Tellis (1993), "Pioneer Advantage: Marketing Logic or Marketing Legend?" *Journal of Marketing Research* 30 (May), 158–70.

Golder, Peter N., and Gerard J. Tellis (1997), "Will It Ever Fly? Modeling the Takeoff of Really New Consumer Durables." *Marketing Science* 16 (3), 256–70.

Graham, Roger C., and Kristina D. Frankenberger (2000), "The Contribution of Changes in Advertising Expenditures to Earnings and Market Values." *Journal of Business Research* 50 (2) (November), 149–55.

Gruca, Thomas S., and Lopo Leotte do Rego (2005), "Customer Satisfaction, Cash Flow, and Shareholder Value." *Journal of Marketing* 69 (July), 115–30.

Gupta, Sunil, and Donald R. Lehmann (2003), "Customers as Assets." *Journal of Interactive Marketing* 17 (1) (Winter), 9–24.

Gupta, Sunil, and Donald R. Lehmann (2005), *Managing Customers as Investments: The Strategic Value of Customers in the Long Run.* Philadelphia, Penn.: Wharton School Publishing.

Gupta, Sunil, Donald R. Lehmann, and Jennifer Ames Stuart (2004), "Valuing Customers." *Journal of Marketing Research* 41 (February), 7–18.

Gupta, Sunil, and Valarie Zeithaml (2006), "Customer Metrics and their Impact on Financial Performance," *Marketing Science,* forthcoming.

Gustafson, Anders, Michael D. Johnson, and Inger Roos (2005), "The Effects of Customer Satisfaction, Relationship Commitment Dimensions, and Triggers on Customer Retention." *Journal of Marketing* 69 (October), 210–8.

Hallowell, Roger (1996), "The Relationships of Customer Satisfaction, Customer Loyalty, and Profitability: An Empirical Study." *International Journal of Service Industry Management* 7 (4), 27–42.

Hauser, John, Gerard J. Tellis, and Abbie Griffin (2006), "Research on Innovation: A Review and Agenda for Marketing Science." *Marketing Science,* forthcoming.

Hendricks, Kevin B., and Vinod R. Singhal (1996), "Quality Awards and the Market Value of the Firm: An Empirical Investigation." *Management Science* 42 (March), 415–36.

Hendricks, Kevin B., and Vinod R. Singhal (1997), "Delays in New Product Introductions and the Market Value of the Firm: The Consequences of Being Late to the Market." *Management Science* 43 (4), 422–36.

Heskett, James L., Thomas O. Jones, Gary W. Loveman, W. Earl Sasser, Jr., and Leonard Schlesinger (1994), "Putting the Service-Profit Chain to Work." *Harvard Business Review* 72 (2), 164–74.

Hirschey, Mark (1982), "Intangible Capital Aspects of Advertising and R&D Expenditures." *Journal of Industrial Economics* 30 (June), 375–90.

Ho, Y.K., H.T. Keh, and J.M. Ong (2005), "The Effects of R&D and Advertising on Firm Value: An Examination of Manufacturing and Non-Manufacturing Firms." *IEEE Transactions on Engineering Management* 52 (1), 3–14.

Hogan, John E., Donald R. Lehmann, Maria Merino, Rajendra K. Srivastava, Jacquelyn S. Thomas, and Peter C. Verhoef (2002), "Linking Customer Assets to Financial Performance." *Journal of Service Research* 5 (1) (August), 26–38.

Hogan, John E., Katherine N. Lemon, and Barak Libai (2003), "What Is the True Value of a Lost Customer?" *Journal of Service Research* 5 (3) (February), 196–208.

Hogan, John E., Katherine N. Lemon, and Roland T. Rust (2002), "Customer Equity Management: Charting New Direction for the Future of Marketing." *Journal of Service Research* 5 (1), 4–12.

Horsky, Dan, and Patrick Swyngedouw (1987), "Does It Pay to Change Your Company's Name? A Stock Market Perspective." *Marketing Science* 6 (4), 320–35.

Houston, M.B., and S. A. Johnson (2000), "Buyer-Supplier Contracts versus Joint Ventures: Determinants and Consequences of Transaction Structure." *Journal of Marketing Research* 37 (February), 1–15.

Howard, John A., and Jagdish Sheth (1969), *The Theory of Buyer Behavior*. New York, N.Y.: John Wiley and Sons.

Ittner, Christopher D., and David F. Larcker (1996), "Measuring the Impact of Quality Initiatives on Firm Financial Performance." In *Advances in the Management of Organizational Quality*, vol. 1, eds. Soumen Ghosh and Donald Fedor, 1–37. Greenwich, Conn.: JAI Press.

Ittner, Christopher, and David Larcker (1998), "Are Non-financial Measures Leading Indicators of Financial Performance? An Analysis of Customer Satisfaction." *Journal of Accounting Research* 36 (Supplement), 1–35.

Jarrell, Gregg, and Sam Peltzman (1985), "The Impact of Product Recalls on the Wealth of Sellers." *Journal of Political Economy* 93 (3), 512–36.

Jose, Manuel L., Len M. Nichols, and Jerry L. Stevens (1986), "Contributions of Diversification, Promotion, and R&D to the Value of Multi Product Firms: A Tobin's *q* Approach." *Financial Management* 15 (4), 33–42.

Joshi, Amit, and Dominique M. Hanssens (2004), "Advertising Spending and Market Capitalization." Cambridge, Mass.: Marketing Science Institute, Report No. 04–110.

Kallapur, Sanjey, and Sabrina Y.S. Kwan (2004), "The Value Relevance and Reliability of Brand Assets Recognized by UK Firms." *Accounting Review* 79 (1) (January), 151–72.

Kalyanaram, Gurumurthy, William T. Robinson, and Glen L. Urban (1995), "Order of Market Entry: Established Empirical Generalizations, Emerging Empirical Generalizations, and Future Research." *Marketing Science* 14 (3, part 2), G212–21.

Kamakura, Wagner A., Vikas Mittal, Fernando de Rosa, and Jose Alfonso Mazzon (2002), "Assessing the Service Profit Chain." *Marketing Science* 21 (3), 294–317.

Kaplan, Robert, and David P. Norton (1996), *The Balanced Scorecard*. Boston, Mass.: Harvard Business School Press.

Keller, Kevin Lane, and Donald R. Lehmann (2003), "The Brand Value Chain: Optimizing Strategic and Financial Brand Performance." *Marketing Management* 12 (3) (May/June), 26–31.

Kerin, Roger A., and Raj Sethuraman (1998), "Exploring the Brand Value-Shareholder Value Nexus for Consumer Goods Companies." *Journal of the Academy of Marketing Science* 26 (4), 260–73.

Kim, Namwoon, Vijay Mahajan, and Rajendra K. Srivastava (1995), "Determining the Going Value of a Business in an Emerging Information Technology Industry: The Case for Cellular Communications Industry." *Technological Forecasting and Social Change* 49 (3) (July), 257–79.

Kirca, Ahmet H., Satish Jayachandran, and William O. Bearden (2005), "Market Orientation: A Meta-Analytic Review and Assessment of its Antecedents and Impact on Performance." *Journal of Marketing* 69 (April), 24–41.

Kirpalani, V.A., and Stanley S. Shapiro (1973), "Financial Dimensions of Marketing Management." *Journal of Marketing* 37 (July), 40–9.

Kohli, Ajay K., and Bernard J. Jaworski (1990), "Market Orientation: The Construct, Research Propositions, and Managerial Implications." *Journal of Marketing* 54 (April), 1–18.

Koku, Paul S., Harsharanjeet S. Jagpal, and P.V. Viswanath (1997), "The Effect of New Product Announcements and Preannouncements on Stock Price." *Journal of Market-Focused Management* 2 (November), 183–99.

Kopalle, Praveen K., and Donald R. Lehmann (2001), "Strategic Management of Expectations: The Role of Disconfirmation Sensitivity and Perfectionism." *Journal of Marketing Research* 38 (August), 386–94.

Lane, Vicki, and Robert Jacobson (1995), "Stock Market Reactions to Brand Extension Announcements: The Effects of Brand Attitude and Familiarity." *Journal of Marketing* 63 (Special Issue), 180–97.

Lehmann, Donald R. (2004), "Linking Marketing to Financial Performance and Firm Value." *Journal of Marketing* 68 (October), 73–5.

Lewis, Michael (2006), "Customer Acquisition Promotion and Customer Asset Value." *Journal of Marketing Research* 43 (May), 195–203.

Lodish, Leonard M., Magid Abraham, S. Kalmenson, J. Livelsberger, Beth Lubetkin, B. Richardson, and M.E. Stevens (1995), "How TV Advertising Works: A Meta-Analysis of 389 Real World Split Cable TV Advertising Experiments." *Journal of Marketing Research* 32 (May), 125–39.

Lusch, Robert F., and Nicholas S.P. Tay (2004), "Agent-Based Modeling: Gaining Insight into Firm and Industry Performance." In *Assessing Marketing Strategy Performance*, eds. Christine Moorman and Donald R. Lehmann, 213–28. Cambridge, Mass.: Marketing Science Institute.

Madden, Thomas J., Frank Fehle, and Susan Fournier (2006), "Brands Matter: An Empirical Demonstration of the Creation of Shareholder Value Through Branding." *Journal of the Academy of Marketing Science* 34 (Spring), 224–35.

Mahajan, Vijay, Vithala R. Rao, and Rajendra K. Srivastava (1994), "An Approach to Assess the Importance of Brand Equity in Acquisition Decisions." *Journal of Product Innovation Management* 11 (3), 221–35.

Matsuno, Ken, John Mentzer, and Aysegul Ozsomer (2002), "The Effects of Entrepreneurial Proclivity and Market Orientation on Business Performance." *Journal of Marketing* 66 (July), 18–32.

Mela, Carl F., Sunil Gupta, and Donald R. Lehmann (1997), "The Long-Term Impact of Promotion and Advertising on Consumer Brand Choice." *Journal of Marketing Research* 34 (May), 248–61.

Mittal, Vikas, Eugene W. Anderson, Akin Sayrak, and Pandu Tadikamalla (2005), "Dual Emphasis and the Long Term Financial Impact of Customer Satisfaction." *Marketing Science* 24 (4), 544–55.

Miyazaki, A.D., and A.G. Morgan (2001), "Assessing Market Value of Event Sponsoring: Corporate Olympic Sponsorships." *Journal of Advertising Research* 41 (January–February), 9–15.

Mizik, Natalie, and Robert Jacobson (2003), "Trading Off Between Value Creation and Value Appropriation: The Financial Implication of Shifts in Strategic Emphasis." *Journal of Marketing* 67 (January), 63–76.

Mizik, Natalie, and Robert Jacobson (2004), "Stock Return Response Modeling." In *Assessing Marketing Strategy Performance*, eds. Christine Moorman and Donald R. Lehmann, 29–46. Cambridge, Mass.: Marketing Science Institute.

Mizik, Natalie, and Robert Jacobson (2006), "Myopic Marketing Management: The Phenomenon and Its Long-term Impact on Firm Value." Cambridge, Mass.: Marketing Science Institute, Report No. 06–100.

Moorman, Christine, Rohit Deshpandé, and Gerald Zaltman (1993), "Factors Affecting Trust in Market Research Relationships." *Journal of Marketing* 57 (January), 81–101.

Moorman, Christine, Gerald Zaltman, and Rohit Deshpandé (1992), "Relationships Between Providers and Users of Market Research: The Dynamics of Trust Within and Between Organizations." *Journal of Marketing Research* 29 (August), 314–29.

Morgan, Neil A., and Lopo Leotte do Rego (2006a), "Brand Portfolio Strategy and Performance." Cambridge, Mass.: Marketing Science Institute, Report 06–101.

Morgan, Neal A., and Lopo Leotte do Rego (2006b), "The Value of Different Customer Satisfaction and Loyalty Metrics in Predicting Business Performance." *Marketing Science*, forthcoming.

Narayanan, Sridhar, Ramarao Desiraju, and Pradeep K. Chintagunta (2004), "Return on Investment Implications for Pharmaceutical Promotional Expenditures: The Role of Marketing Mix Interactions." *Journal of Marketing* 68 (October), 90–105.

Narver, John C., and Stanley F. Slater (1990), "The Effect of a Market Orientation on Business Profitability." *Journal of Marketing* 54 (October), 20–35.

Nayyar, Praveen P. (1995), "Stock Market Reaction to Customer Service Changes." *Strategic Management Journal* 16 (January), 39–54.

Neslin, Scott A. (2002), *Sales Promotion*. Cambridge, Mass.: Marketing Science Institute.

Oliver, Richard (1980), "A Cognitive Model of the Antecedents and Consequences of Satisfaction Decisions." *Journal of Marketing Research* 17 (November) 460-9.

Parasuraman, A., Valarie A. Zeithaml, and Leonard L. Berry (1988), "SERVQUAL: A Multiple-Item Scale for Measuring Consumer Perceptions of Service Quality." *Journal of Retailing* 64 (Spring), 12–40.

Pardue, J. Harold, Eric Higgins, and Tim Biggart (2000), "The Impact of New Product Announcements on Firm Value in Information Technology Producing Industries: An Examination of Industry-Level Evolutionary Eras." *The Engineering Economist* 45 (2), 144–57.

Pauwels, Koen, Jorge Silva-Risso, Shuba Srinivasan, and Dominique M. Hanssens (2004), "New Products, Sales Promotions, and Firm Value: The Case of the Automobile Industry." *Journal of Marketing* 68 (October), 142–56.

Pelham, Alfred M. (1999), "Influence of Environment, Strategy, and Market Orientation on Performance in Small Manufacturing Firms." *Journal of Business Research* 45 (1), 33–46.

Pelham, Alfred M., and David T. Wilson (1996), "A Longitudinal Study of the Impact of Market Structure, Firm Structure, Strategy, and Market Orientation Culture on Dimensions of Small Firm Performance." *Journal of the Academy of Market Science* 24 (1), 27–43.

Ramaswami, Sridhar N., Mukesh Bhargava, and Rajendra Srivastava (2004), "Market-Based Assets and Capabilities, Business Processes, and Financial Performance." Cambridge, Mass.: Marketing Science Institute, Report No. 04–102.

Randall, Taylor, Karl Ulrich, and David Reibstein (1998), "Brand Equity and Product Line Extent." *Marketing Science* 17 (4), 356–79.

Rao, Vithala R., Manoj K. Agrawal, and Denise Dahlhoff (2004), "How Is Manifest Branding Strategy Related to the Intangible Value of a Corporation?" *Journal of Marketing* 68 (October), 126–41.

Reibstein, David J., and Paul Farris (1995), "Market Share and Distribution: A Generalization, a Speculation and Some Implications." *Marketing Science: Special Issue on Empirical Generalizations in Marketing* 14 (3, part 2), 190–202.

Reibstein, David J., Yogesh Joshi, David Norton, and Paul Farris (2005), "Marketing Dashboards: A Decision Support System for Assessing Marketing Productivity." Philadelphia, Penn.: University of Pennsylvania, Wharton School, Working Paper.

Reichheld, Frederick F. (2001), *Loyalty Rules!: How Today's Leaders Build Lasting Relationships.* Cambridge, Mass.: Harvard Business School Publishing.

Reichheld, Frederick F., and Thomas Teal (1996), *The Loyalty Effect.* Boston, Mass.: Harvard Business School Press.

Reinartz, Werner, Manfred Krafft, and Wayne D. Hoyer (2004), "The Customer Relationship Management Process: Its Measurement and Impact on Performance." *Journal of Marketing Research* 61 (August), 293–305.

Reinartz, Werner, and V. Kumar (2000), "On the Profitability of Long-Life Customers in a Noncontractual Setting: An Empirical Investigation and Implications for Marketing." *Journal of Marketing* 64 (October), 17–35.

Reinartz, Werner J., Jacquelyn S. Thomas, and V. Kumar (2005), "Balancing Acquisition and Retention Resources to Maximize Customer Profitability." *Journal of Marketing* 69 (January), 63–79.

Rindfleisch, Aric, Alan Malter, Shankar Ganesan, and Christine Moorman (2004), "Cross-Sectional vs. Longitudinal New Product Outcomes." Tucson, Ariz.: University of Arizona, Working Paper.

Riskey, Dwight R. (1997), "How T.V. Advertising Works: An Industry Response." *Journal of Marketing Research* 34 (May), 292–3.

Rust, Roland, Katherine Lemon, and Valarie Zeithaml (2004), "Return on Marketing: Using Customer Equity to Focus Marketing Strategy." *Journal of Marketing* 68 (January), 109–26.

Rust, Roland T., Christine Moorman, and Peter R. Dickson (2002), "Getting Return on Quality: Cost Reduction, Revenue Expansion, or Both?" *Journal of Marketing* 66 (October), 7–24.

Rust, Roland, Anthony Zahorik, and Timothy Keiningham (1995), "Return on Quality (ROQ): Making Service Quality Financially Accountable." *Journal of Marketing* 59 (April), 58–70.

Rust, Roland T., Valarie A. Zeithaml, and Katherine N. Lemon (2000), *Driving Customer Equity: How Customer Lifetime Value is Reshaping Corporate Strategy.* New York, N.Y.: Free Press.

Schmittlein, David, Donald Morrison, and Richard Colombo (1987), "Counting Your Customers: Who Are They and What Will They Do Next?" *Management Science* 33 (1) (January), 1–24.

Seiders, Kathleen, Glenn B. Voss, Dhruv Grewal, and Andrea Godfrey (2005), "Do Satisfied Customers Buy More: Examining Moderating Influences in a Retailing Context." *Journal of Marketing* 69 (October), 26–43.

Sethuraman, Raj, and Gerard J. Tellis (1991), "An Analysis of the Tradeoff Between Advertising and Price Discounting." *Journal of Marketing Research* 28 (2) (May), 160–74.

Simon, Carol J., and Mary W. Sullivan (1993), "The Measurement and Determinants of Brand Equity: A Financial Approach." *Marketing Science* 12 (Winter), 28–52.

Slater, Stanley F., and John C. Narver (1994), "Does Competitive Environment Moderate the Market Orientation-Performance Relationship?" *Journal of Marketing* 58 (January), 46–55.

Sorescu, Alina B., Rajesh Chandy, and Jaideep Prabhu (2003), "Sources and Financial Consequences of Radical Innovation: Insights from Pharmaceuticals." *Journal of Marketing* 67 (October), 82–102.

Srinivasan, Raji, and Sundar Bharadwaj (2004), "Event Studies in Marketing Strategy Research." In *Assessing Marketing Strategy Performance*, eds. Christine Moorman and Donald R. Lehmann, 9–28. Cambridge, Mass.: Marketing Science Institute.

Srinivasan, Raji, Arvind Rangaswamy, and Gary L. Lilien (2005), "Turning Adversity into Advantage: Does Proactive Marketing During a Recession Pay Off?" *International Journal of Research in Marketing* 22 (2) (June), 109–25.

Srivastava, Rajendra, Liam Fahey, and H. Kurt Christensen (2001), "The Resource-Based View and Marketing: The Role of Market-Based Assets in Gaining Competitive Advantage." *Journal of Management* 27, 777–802.

Srivastava, Rajendra K., Tasadduq A. Shervani, and Liam Fahey (1998), "Market-Based Assets and Shareholder Value: A Framework for Analysis." *Journal of Marketing* 62 (January), 2–18.

Steiner, Robert L. (1973), "Does Advertising Lower Consumer Prices?" *Journal of Marketing* 37 (October), 19.

Stewart, David W., and David H. Furse (1986), *Effective Television Advertising: A Study of 1000 Commercials*. Lexington, Mass.: Lexington Books.

Sultan, Fareena, John U. Farley, and Donald R. Lehmann (1990), "A Meta-Analysis of Applications of Diffusion Models." *Journal of Marketing Research* 27 (February), 70–7.

Szymanski, David M., Lisa C. Troy, and Sundar G. Bharadwaj (1995), "Order of Entry and Business Performance: An Empirical Synthesis and Reexamination." *Journal of Marketing* 59 (October), 17–33.

Tellis, Gerard J., Stefan Stremersch, and Eden Yin (2003), "The International Takeoff of New Products: Economics, Culture, and Country Innovativeness." *Marketing Science* 22 (2), 188–208.

Verhoef, Peter C. (2003), "Understanding the Effect of Customer Relationship Management Efforts on Customer Retention and Customer Share Development." *Journal of Marketing* 67 (October), 30–45.

Villanueva, Julian, Shijin Yoo, and Dominique M. Hanssens (2003), "The Impact of Acquisition Channels on Customer Equity." Barcelona and Madrid, Spain: IESE Business School, Working Paper No. 516.

Winer, Russell S. (2000), "What Marketing Metrics Are Used by MSI Members?" In "Marketing Metrics" prepared by Marion Debruyne and Katrina Hubbard. Cambridge, Mass.: Marketing Science Institute, Report 00–119.

Zeithaml, Valarie A. (2000), "Service Quality, Profitability, and the Economic Worth of Customers: What We Know and What We Need to Learn." *Journal of the Academy of Marketing Science* 28 (1), 67–85.

Zeithaml, Valarie A., and A. Parasuraman (2004), *Service Quality*. Cambridge, Mass.: Marketing Science Institute.

For Further Reading

Aaker, David W., and James M. Carman (1982), "Are You Over Advertising?" *Journal of Advertising Research* 22, 57–70.

Abela, Andrew, Bruce H. Clark, and Tim Ambler (2004), "Marketing Performance Measurement, Performance, and Learning." *Marketing Management* 15 (3), 18–23.

Abraham, Magid H., and Leonard M. Lodish (1990), "Getting the Most Out of Advertising and Promotion." *Harvard Business Review* 90 (3), 50–8.

Allenby, Greg, and Dominique Hanssens (2004), "Advertising Response." Cambridge, Mass.: Marketing Science Institute, Report No. 05–200a.

Ambler, Tim, and Flora Kokkinaki (2000), "Marketing Performance Measurement: Which Way Is Up?" *International Journal of Business Performance Management* 2 (1–3), 72–85.

Ambler, Tim, and Chris Styles (1995), "Brand Equity: Toward Measures that Matter." London, U.K.: London Business School, Centre for Marketing, Working Paper No. 95–902.

Anderson, Eugene W., and V. Mittal (2000), "Strengthening the Satisfaction-Profit Chain." *Journal of Service Research* 3 (2), 107–20.

Barwise, Patrick, and Alany Styler (2002), *Marketing Expenditure Trends*. London, U.K.: London Business School.

Bayus, Barry, Gary Erickson, and Robert Jacobson (2003), "The Financial Rewards of New-product Introductions in the Personal Computer Industry." *Management Science* 49 (2), 197–210.

Berger, Paul D., Ruth N. Bolton, Douglas Bowman, Elten Briggs, V. Kumar, A. Parasuraman, and Creed Terry (2002), "Marketing Actions and the Value of Customer Assets: A Framework for Customer Asset Management." *Journal of Service Research* 5 (1) (August), 39–54.

Blattberg, Robert C., and Stephen J. Hoch (1990), "Database Models and Managerial Intuition: 50% Model + 50% Manager." *Management Science* 36 (8), 887–99.

Bolton, Ruth N., P.K. Kannan, and Matthew Bramlett (2000), "Implications of Loyalty Program Membership and Service Experiences for Customer Retention and Value." *Journal of the Academy of Marketing Science* 28 (1), 95–108.

Brady, Diane, and David Kiley (2004), "Making Marketing Measure Up." *Business Week* (December 13), 112–3.

Chaudhuri, Arjun (2002), "How Brand Reputation Affects the Advertising-Brand Equity Link." *Journal of Advertising Research* 42 (May/June), 33–43.

Christen, Markus, Sachin Gupta, John C. Porter, Richard Staelin, and Dick R. Wittink (1994), "Using Market-Level Data to Understand Promotion Effects in a Nonlinear Model." *Journal of Marketing Research* 34 (August), 322–34.

Clark, Bruce H., Andrew V. Abela, and Tim Ambler (2004), "Return on Measurement: Relating Marketing Metrics Practices to Strategic Performance." Unpublished paper.

Cleland, Alan S., and Albert V. Bruno (1996), *Market Value Process: Bridging Customer and Shareholder Value*. San Francisco, Calif.: Jossey-Bass Publishers.

Dekimpe, Marnik, and Dominique Hanssens (1995), "The Persistence of Marketing Effects on Sales." *Marketing Science* 14 (1), 1–21.

Duffy, Mike (2000), "Kraft's Return on Marketing Investment: Portfolio Planning Implications. In "Marketing Metrics" prepared by Marion Debruyne and Katrina Hubbard. Cambridge, Mass.: Marketing Science Institute, Report 00–119.

Farris, Paul W., David Reibstein, and Ervin Shames (1998), "Advertising Budgeting: A Report from the Field." New York, N.Y.: American Association of Advertising Agencies.

Fornell, Claes, David VanAmburg, Forrest Morgeson, Eugene E. Anderson, Barbara Everitt Bryant, and Michael D. Johnson (2005), "The American Customer Satisfaction Index at Ten Years, A Summary of Findings: Implications for the Economy, Stock Returns and Management." Ann Arbor, Mich.: University of Michigan, Stephen M. Ross School of Business.

Forrester, Jay W. (1961), "Advertising: A Problem in Industrial Dynamics." *Harvard Business Review* (March–April), 110.

Forrester, Jay W. (1965), "Modeling of Market and Company Interactions." In *Marketing and Economic Development,* ed. Peter D. Bennet, 353–64. Chicago, Ill.: American Marketing Association.

Greenley, Gordon E. (1995), "Market Orientation and Company Performance: Empirical Evidence from UK Companies." *British Journal of Management* 6, 1–13.

Greyser, Stephen, A. (1980), "Marketing Issues." *Journal of Marketing* 47 (Winter), 89–93.

Han, Jin K., Namwoon Kim, and Rajendra K. Srivastava (1998), "Marketing Orientation and Organizational Performance: Is Innovation a Missing Link?" *Journal of Marketing* 62 (October), 30–45.

Harris, Lloyd C. (2001), "Market Orientation and Performance: Objective and Subjective Empirical Evidence from UK Companies." *Journal of Management Studies* 38 (1), 17–43.

Harris, Lloyd C., and Emmanual Ogbonna (2001), "Strategic Human Resource Management, Market Orientation, and Organizational Performance." *Journal of Business Research* 51, 157–66.

Hauser, John, and Gerald Katz (1998), "Metrics: You Are What You Measure." *European Management Journal* 16 (5), 517–28.

Hawkins, Del I., Roger J. Best, and Charles M. Lillis (1987), "The Nature and Measurement of Marketing Productivity in Consumer Durables Industries: A Firm Level Analysis." *Journal of Academy of Marketing Science* 1 (Winter) (4), 1–8.

Homburg, Christian, and Christian Pflesser (2000), "A Multiple-Layer Model of Market-Oriented Organizational Culture: Measurement Issues and Performance Outcomes." *Journal of Marketing Research* 37 (November), 449–62.

Jaworski, Bernard J., and Ajay Kohli (1993), "Marketing Orientation: Antecedents and Consequences." *Journal of Marketing* 57 (July), 53–70.

Kamakura, Wagner A., and Gary J. Russell (1993), "Measuring Brand Value with Scanner Data." *International Journal of Research in Marketing (Special Issue on Brand Equity)* 10 (March), 9–22.

Kaul, Anil, and Dick R. Wittink (1995), "Empirical Generalizations about the Impact of Advertising on Price Sensitivity and Price." *Marketing Science* 14 (3), G151–60.

Keller, Kevin Lane (2002), *Strategic Brand Management*, 2nd ed. Upper Saddle River, N.J.: Prentice Hall.

Keller, Kevin Lane, and Donald R. Lehmann (2005), "Brands and Branding: Research Findings and Future Priorities." Cambridge, Mass.: Marketing Science Institute, Report No. 05-200b.

Kopalle, Praveen K., and Donald R. Lehmann (1995), "The Effects of Advertised and Observed Quality on Expectations about New Product Quality." *Journal of Marketing Research* 32 (August), 280–90.

Kumar, Pryash (1999), "The Impact of Long-Term Client Relationships on the Performance of Business Service Firms." *Journal of Services Research* 2 (August), 4–18.

Lee, P. Ruby, and Rajdeep Grewal (2003), "Strategic Response to New Technologies and Their Impact on Firm Performance." *Journal of Marketing* 68 (October), 157–71.

Lehmann, Donald R. (2006), "The Metrics Imperative: Making Marketing Matter." In *Review of Marketing Research*, vol. 2, ed. Narish Malhotra, 177–202. Armonk, N.Y.: M. E. Sharpe.

Lehmann, Donald R., and Russell S. Winer (2005), *Product Management*. Englewood Cliffs, N.J.: Prentice-Hall.

Little, John D.C. (1970), "Models and Managers: The Concept of a Decision Calculus." *Management Science* 16 (8), b-466–b-484, b-485.

Lodish, Leonard M. (1997), "J.P. Jones and M.H. Blair on Measuring Advertising Effects—Another Point of View." *Journal of Advertising Research* (September–October), 75–9.

Loveman, Gary W. (1998), "Employee Satisfaction, Customer Loyalty, and Financial Performance: An Empirical Examination of the Service Profit Chain in Retail Banking." *Journal of Service Research* 1 (1), 18–31.

Mathur, Lynette K., and Ike Mathur (1995), "The Effect of Advertising Slogan Changes on the Market Values of Firms." *Journal of Advertising Research* 35 (1), 59–65.

Mathur, Lynette Knowles, Ike Mathur, and Nanda Rangan (1997), "The Wealth Effects Associated with a Celebrity Endorser: The Michael Jordan Phenomenon." *Journal of Advertising Research* (May), 67–73.

McGovern, Gail J., David Court, John A. Quelch, and Blair Crawford (2004), "Bringing Customers into the Boardroom." *Harvard Business Review* (November), 70–80.

Merino, Maria, Raji Srinivasan, and Rajendra Srivastava (2003), "Impact of Advertising on Business Performance and Volatility." Working Paper.

Meyer, Christopher (1994), "How the Right Measures Help Teams Excel." *Harvard Business Review* (May–June), 95–103.

Moorman, Christine, and Donald R. Lehmann (2004), *Assessing Marketing Strategy Performance*. Cambridge, Mass.: Marketing Science Institute.

Much, James G., Lee S. Sproull, and Michal Tamuz (1989), "Learning from Samples of One or Fewer." *Organizational Science* 2 (1) (February), 1–12.

Murphy, Allan H., and Barbara G. Brown (1984), "A Comparative Evaluation of Objective and Subjective Weather Forecasts in the United States." *Journal of Forecasting* 3, 369–93.

Nelson, Eugene, Roland T. Rust, Anthony Zahorik, Robin L. Rose, Paul Batalden, and Beth Siemanski (1992), "Do Patient Perceptions of Quality Relate to Hospital Financial Performance?" *Journal of Healthcare Marketing* (December), 1–13.

Nijs, Vincent R., Marnik G. Dekimpe, Jan-Benedict E.M. Steenkamp, and Dominique M. Hanssens (2001), "The Category-Demand Effects of Price Promotions." *Marketing Science* 20 (1), 1–22.

Oliver, Richard (1997), *Satisfaction: A Behavioral Perspective on the Consumer.* New York, N.Y.: McGraw-Hill.

Parasuraman, A., Valarie A. Zeithaml, and Leonard L. Berry (1994), "Reassessment of Expectations as a Comparison Standard in Measuring Service Quality: Implications for Further Research." *Journal of Marketing* 58 (January), 111–24.

Reibstein, David J., and Raj Srivastava (2005), "Metrics for Linking Marketing to Financial Performance." Cambridge, Mass.: Marketing Science Institute, Report No. 05-200e.

Reinartz, Werner J., and V. Kumar (2004), "A Customer Lifetime Value Framework for Customer Selection and Optimal Resource Allocation Strategy." *Journal of Marketing* 68 (October), 106–25.

Rucci, Anthony, Steven Kirn, and Richard Quinn (1998), "The Employee-Customer-Profit Chain at Sears." *Harvard Business Review* (January–February), 83–97.

Rust, Roland T., Tim Ambler, Gregory S. Carpenter, V. Kumar, and Rajendra K. Srivastava (2004), "Measuring Marketing Productivity: Current Knowledge and Future Directions." *Journal of Marketing* 68 (October), 76–89.

Rust, Roland, and Anthony Zahorik (1993), "Customer Satisfaction, Customer Retention, and Market Share." *Journal of Retailing* 69 (Summer), 193–215.

Sethuraman, Raj (1995), "A Meta-Analysis of National Brand and Store Brand Cross-Promotional Price Elasticities." *Marketing Letters* 6 (4), 275–86.

Sheth, Jagdish N., and Rajendra S. Sisodia (2002), "Marketing Productivity Issues and Analysis." *Journal of Business Research* 55 (5) (May), 349–62.

Srivastava, Rajendra, T.H. Moinesh, R. Wood, and A.J. Caprano (1999), "The Value of Corporate Reputation: Evidence from the Equity Market." *Corporate Reputation Review* 1 (1), 62–8.

Tellis, Gerard J., and Doyle L. Weiss (1995), "Does TV Advertising Really Affect Sales? The Role of Measures, Models, and Data Aggregation." *Journal of Advertising Research* 24 (3) (Fall), 1–12.

Vakratsas, Demetrios, and Tim Ambler (1999), "How Advertising Works: What Do We Really Know?" *Journal of Marketing* 63 (January), 26–43.

ABOUT THE AUTHORS

Donald R. Lehmann is the George E. Warren Professor of Business at the Columbia Business School. He was Executive Director of the Marketing Science Institute from 1993–95 and again from 2001–03, and serves on the Executive Directors Council.

His research interests include modeling individual and group decision making, assessing marketing productivity, measuring and managing marketing assets (i.e., customers and brands), the introduction and adoption of innovations, and meta-analysis. He has taught courses in marketing, management, and statistics.

He has published in and served on the editorial boards of the *Journal of Consumer Research*, *Journal of Marketing*, *Journal of Marketing Research*, *Management Science*, and *Marketing Science*, and is founding editor of *Marketing Letters*. In addition to MSI working papers and numerous journal articles, he has published four books: *Market Research and Analysis*, *Analysis for Marketing Planning*, *Product Management*, and *Meta-Analysis in Marketing*. He is the editor (with Christine Moorman) of *Assessing Marketing Strategy Performance* (MSI 2004). He was president of the Association for Consumer Research in 1995.

In September 2006, he was awarded the American Marketing Association's Charles Coolidge Parlin Award and was named a Fellow of the Association for Consumer Research.

Other awards include the 2004 Harold H. Maynard Award (with Kusum Ailawadi and Scott Neslin), the 2000 Paul D. Converse Award, the 1995 William F. O'Dell Award (with Fareena Sultan and John Farley), and the 2002 William F. O'Dell Award (with Carl Mela and Sunil Gupta). In 1999, he received the AMA/Irwin/McGraw-Hill Distinguished Marketing Educator Award.

He has a B.S. degree in mathematics from Union College, Schenectady, New York, and an M.S.I.A. and Ph.D. from the Krannert Graduate School of Management, Purdue University.

David J. Reibstein is the William S. Woodside Professor and Professor of Marketing at The Wharton School, University of Pennsylvania. From 1987–92, he was the Julian Aresty Professor of Marketing, Vice Dean, and Director of the Wharton Graduate Division of the University of Pennsylvania. He was Executive Director of the Marketing Science Institute from 1999–2001 and serves on the Executive Directors Council.

Previously, he was Assistant Professor of Marketing at the Harvard Business School (1975) and a Visiting Professor of Marketing at INSEAD at Fontainebleau, France (1983) and at Stanford University (1987). He has received a teaching award at Wharton every year he has taught there since 1982. He currently runs an executive program he developed on "Linking Marketing Metrics to Financial Performance."

His research interests are in marketing ROI, Internet marketing, competitive marketing strategy, market segmentation, marketing models, and understanding brand choice behavior.

He has recently coauthored the book, *Marketing Metrics: 50+ Metrics Every Manager Should Master*. He also co-edited *Wharton on Dynamic Competitive Strategy*, and is co-author of *Marketing: Concepts, Strategies and Decisions, Strategy Analysis with Value War,* and *Cases in Marketing Research*. He has authored numerous articles in journals including the *Journal of Marketing Research, Marketing Science, Harvard Business Review, Journal of Advertising Research, Journal of Marketing*, and *Journal of Consumer Research*.

In 2005, he was the recipient of Purdue University's Distinguished Alumni Award. He received his Ph.D. in industrial administration at Purdue University, he was in the M.B.A. program at Tulane University, and obtained his B.A. in statistics and political science and B.S. in business administration at the University of Kansas. He received an honorary master's degree from the University of Pennsylvania.

ABOUT MSI

Founded in 1961, the Marketing Science Institute is a learning organization dedicated to bridging the gap between marketing science theory and business practice. MSI currently brings together executives from approximately 70 sponsoring corporations with leading researchers from over 100 universities worldwide.

As a nonprofit institution, MSI financially supports academic research for the development—and practical translation—of leading-edge marketing knowledge on topics of importance to business. Issues of key importance to business performance are identified by the Board of Trustees, which represents MSI corporations and the academic community. MSI supports studies by academics on these issues and disseminates the results through conferences and workshops, as well as through its publications series.

Related MSI Working Papers

Report No.

86-105 "Measurement and Use of Market Response Functions for Allocating Marketing Resources" by Vithala R. Rao and Darius J. Sabavala

Reviews and synthesizes the literature on measuring market response functions and marketing-mix decisions over time; proposes an innovative approach for measuring resources.

88-109 "Discontinuities, Value Delivery, and the Share-Return Association: A Re-Examination of the 'Share-Causes-Profits' Controversy" by Cathy Anterasian and Lynn W. Phillips

Develops a view of competitive advantage based upon superior value delivery to customers and outlines linkages among value delivery, competitive advantage, discontinuities, market share, and profits.

88-112 "Valuing Market Strategies" by George S. Day and Liam Fahey

Description of the valuation process and a critique of the benefits and limitations in practice.

89-105 "The Impact of New Product Introductions on the Market Value of Firms" by Paul K. Chaney, Timothy M. Devinney, and Russell S. Winer

Demonstrates the usefulness of a financial economics technique—event study methodology—in a marketing application.

89-118 "Accounting for the Market Share-ROI Relationship" by Paul W. Farris, Mark E. Parry, and Frederick E. Webster, Jr.

Illustrates a method for using accounting identities in the analysis and interpretation of studies dealing with market share-ROI relationships.

89-120 "The Effect of Market Orientation on Business Profitability" by John C. Narver and Stanley F. Slater

Develops a measure of market orientation and a test for the relationship between a business's market orientation and profitability.

91-100 "Shared Marketing Programs and the Performance of Different Business Strategies" by Robert W. Ruekert and Orville C. Walker, Jr.

Examines whether sharing resources increases growth and return on investment for businesses characterized by a "defender" rather than a "prospector" strategy.

91-119 "Recognizing and Measuring Brand Assets" by Peter H. Farquhar, Julia Y. Han, and Yuji Ijiri

Suggests method for formally valuing brands and recognizing them as assets in financial statements. This approach relies on "momentum accounting."

92-104 "Market Orientation: Antecedents and Consequences" by Bernard J. Jaworski and Ajay K. Kohl

Presents findings from two cross-sectional mail surveys designed to measure market orientation, its antecedents, and consequences; discusses the effect of market orientation on business performance.

92-116 "A Financial Approach to Estimating Firm-Level Brand Equity and Measuring the Impact of Marketing Events" by Carol J. Simon and Mary Sullivan

Presents a technique for estimating a firm's brand equity that is based on the financial market value of the firm.

92-118 "Market Orientation, Performance, and the Moderating Influence of Competitive Environment" by Stanley F. Slater and John C. Narver

Tests for moderator effects of a business's market environment on the relationship between market orientation and performance.

92-131 "Market Value of Trademarks Measured via Trademark Litigation" by Sanjai Bhagat and U.N. Umesh

Relates the stock returns of firms to the filing of trademark infringement lawsuits; evaluates average returns of plaintiff and defendant firms.

93-112 "Economic Consequences of Providing Quality and Customer Satisfaction" by Eugene W. Anderson, Claes Fornell, and Donald R. Lehmann

By investigating links between customer-based measures of firm performance and traditional accounting measures of economic returns, demonstrates the economic benefits of increasing customer satisfaction.

93-117 "Market Share and ROI: A Peek at Some Unobserved Variables" by Kusum L. Ailawadi, Paul W. Farris, and Mark E. Parry

Examines the role of unobserved variables on the relationship between market share and profitability; suggests the strategic implications for marketers of better understanding these variables.

93-121 "Market Orientation and Business Performance: An Analysis of Panel Data" by John C. Narver, Robert Jacobson, and Stanley F. Slater

Investigates the effect of market orientation on sales growth and ROI; assesses the effectiveness of panel data analysis in evaluating the relationship between market orientation and business performance.

94-106 "Return on Quality (ROQ): Making Service Quality Financially Accountable" by Roland T. Rust, Anthony J. Zahorik, and Timothy L. Keiningham

Describes a tool that managers can use to evaluate quality improvement expenditures as investments rather than as costs, thus helping them determine which aspects of quality are most worthy of resource allocation.

95-102 "Does Market Orientation Matter for Small Firms?" by Alfred M. Pelham and David T. Wilson

Develops and tests an integrated model of the influence of market orientation on small firm profitability using longitudinal data.

96-121 "Metrics to Value R&D: An Annotated Bibliography" by John R. Hauser

Provides an annotated bibliography for 153 articles in the R&D, marketing, and economics literature; offers a sampling of viewpoints on the "state of the art" on R&D metrics.

97-102 "Sustained Spending and Persistent Response: A New Look at Long-term Marketing Profitability" by Marnik G. Dekimpe and Dominique M. Hanssens

Outlines four possible strategic scenarios for product markets, and proposes a measure of long-term marketing effectiveness. Tests this measure using data from the packaged food and pharmaceuticals industries.

97-104 "Information Search Style and Business Performance in Dynamic and Stable Enviornments: An Exploratory Study" by Stanley F. Slater and John C. Narver

Investigates the relationship between different modes of information search behavior (market-focused information search, learning from others, experimentation, and learning from experience) and business performance in the electronics and paint-manufacturing industries.

97-107 "Market Orientation in U.S. and Scandinavian Companies: A Cross-cultural Study" by Fred Selnes, Bernard J. Jaworski, and Ajay K. Kohli

Examines how a country context affects the organizational factors that drive a market orientation, the levels of market orientation, and the strength of linkages between market orientation and its antecedents and consequences. Suggests that the core framework for market orientation proposed in earlier U.S.-based work generalizes to Scandinavia.

97-108 "Factors Affecting Organizational Performance: A Five-country Comparison" by Rohit Deshpandé, John U. Farley, and Frederick E. Webster, Jr.

Investigates how organizational culture and climate, customer orientation, and innovativeness affect performance in firms in the U.S., England, France, Germany, and Japan. Finds that successful firms transcend national culture differences to develop common drivers of business performance.

97-117 "Research, Development, and Engineering Metrics" by John R. Hauser

Suggests that metrics-based evaluation and management of research, development and engineering should vary based on type of R, D, & E activity (i.e., applied projects, development of core technologies, or basic research). Uses interviews at 10 research-intensive organizations, literature review, and formal mathematical models to develop insights.

97-119 "Market-based Assets and Shareholder Value: A Framework for Analysis" by Rajendra K. Srivastava, Tasadduq A. Shervani, and Liam Fahey

Develops a framework explicating marketing's relationship to market-based assets—such as customer, channel, and partner relationships—that can increase shareholder value through accelerating and enhancing cash flows, reducing volatility and vulnerability, and increasing residual value of cash flows.

98-103 "Commercial Adoption of Advances in the Analysis of Scanner Data" by Randolph E. Bucklin and Sunil Gupta

Examines the commercial use and adoption of state-of-the-art methods of analyzing UPC scanner data by the consumer packaged goods industry in the U.S.

98-132 "Managing Advertising and Promotion for Long-run Profitability" by Kamel Jedidi, Carl F. Mela, and Sunil Gupta

Examines short- and long-term effects of promotions and advertising on consumers' purchase behavior (choice and quantity) and, thus, on long-run profitability. Tests model using eight years of panel data.

99-114 "Marketing Performance Assessment: An Exploratory Investigation into Current Practice and the Role of Firm Orientation" by Flora Kokkinaki and Tim Ambler

Uses interview and survey data to explore how British firms assess their marketing performance; examines the influence both of customer and competitor orientation and of measurement practice on marketing performance.

99-119 "Success in High Technology Markets: Is Marketing Capability Critical?" by Shantanu Dutta, Om Narasimhan, and Surendra Rajiv

Using archival data, develops a framework that estimates a firm's specific capabilities in marketing, manufacturing, and R&D, and how these capabilities affect profitability.

99-126 "Improving Advertising Budgeting" edited by Stephen A. Greyser and H. Paul Root

Summarizes presentations and group discussion sessions of conference on the MAX program of Managing Advertising Expenditures for Financial Performance (a collaboration of MSI and the American Association of Advertising Agencies with the support of the Advertising Research Foundation).

00-111 "Towards a System for Monitoring Brand Health from Store Scanner Data" by C.B. Bhattacharya and Leonard M. Lodish

Defines brand health according to two dimensions—current wellbeing and resistance—and identifies a variety of measures managers can use to track it. Uses longitudinal, store-week data for two product categories.

00-116 "Total Market Orientation, Business Performance, and Innovation" by John C. Narver, Stanley F. Slater, and Douglas L. MacLachlan

Using sample of 41 business units, develops measure of proactive market orientation, and refines measure of reactive market orientation; analyzes the relationships between reactive, proactive, and total market orientation and business performance and innovation.

00-119 "Marketing Metrics" prepared by Marion Debruyne and Katrina Hubbard

Summarizes the proceedings of the Marketing Science Institute's conference on "Marketing Metrics" held October 5–6, 2000, in Toronto, Canada. Offers highlights from ten presentations on the current state of knowledge and practice regarding marketing metrics.

00-120 "Getting Returns from Service Quality: Is the Conventional Wisdom Wrong?" by Roland T. Rust, Christine Moorman, and Peter R. Dickson

Uses survey of managers and secondary data across industries to examine the impact on customer relationship and financial outcomes of service quality improvements that (1) emphasize revenue expansion, (2) emphasize efficiency and cost reduction, and (3) emphasize both revenue expansion and cost reduction simultaneously.

00-500 "Marketing Metrics: A Review of Performance Measures in Use in the U.K. and Spain" by Tim Ambler and Debra Riley

Explores how firms assess their marketing performance, together with differences by industry sector, firm size and nationality (the U.K. and Spain).

01-108 "Driving Customer Equity: Linking Customer Lifetime Value to Strategic Marketing" by Roland T. Rust, Katherine N. Lemon, and Valarie A. Zeithaml

Develops a "Customer Equity" framework based on the concept of customer lifetime value that offers a set of metrics enabling a company to project and quantify the financial impact of marketing expenditures.

01-101 "Tigers and Dragons: Profiling High Performance Asian Firms" by Rohit Deshpandé

Examines how four organizational factors—innovation, market orientation, organizational culture, and organizational climate—affect business performance in six business-to-business firms in cities in six Asian countries.

01-119 "Valuing Customers" by Sunil Gupta, Donald R. Lehmann, and Jennifer Ames Stuart

Develops an approach to value the current and future customer base of a company using customer lifetime value, the discounted future income stream based on acquisition, retention, and expansion projections, and their associated costs.

01-120 "Do Promotions Benefit Manufacturers, Retailers, or Both?" by Shuba Srinivasan, Koen Pauwels, Dominique Hanssens, and Marnik Dekimpe

Using scanner data for 25 product categories over eight years, examines the effects of price promotions on manufacturer revenues and retailer revenues and margins.

02-102 "A Product-Market-Based Measure of Brand Equity" by Kusum L. Ailawadi, Donald R. Lehmann, and Scott A. Neslin

Proposes a product-market-level measure of brand equity; examines its behavior for brands in 23 packaged goods categories over seven years.

02-108 "What Is the True Value of a Lost Customer?" by John E. Hogan, Katherine N. Lemon, and Barak Libai

Incorporates social effects such as word-of-mouth into customer profitability framework; develops a method for estimating the effect of disadoptions on the value of a lost customer. Demonstrates how customer profitability changes over the product lifecycle.

02-114 "Trading Off Value Creation and Value Appropriation: The Financial Implications of Shifts in Strategic Emphasis" by Natalie Mizik and Robert Jacobson

Develops a measure of a firm's strategic emphasis on value appropriation versus value creation and assesses the effect that changes in this measure have on stock return; examines the extent to which this effect is moderated by firm financial situation, past strategic choices, and technological environment.

02-119 "Measuring Marketing Productivity: Linking Marketing to Financial Returns" prepared by Suleyman Cem Bahadir and Kapil R. Tuli

Summarizes the proceedings of MSI conference on "Measuring Marketing Productivity: Linking Marketing to Financial Returns" held October 3–4, 2002, in Dallas, Texas.

02-123 "Superiority in Customer Relationship Management: Consequences for Competitive Advantage and Performance" by George S. Day and Christophe Van den Bulte

Draws on a resource-based view of the firm to specify a customer-relating capability (comprising firm orientation, information, and configuration components), and investigates its effects on sales growth, customer retention, and profitability.

03-106 "Customer Satisfaction, Cash Flow, and Shareholder Value" by Thomas S. Gruca and Lopo Leotte do Rego

Examines the impact of customer satisfaction on future cash flow and cash-flow variability for the firm; also examines whether market concentration or firm size explain differences.

03-109 "Marketing's Impact on Firm Value: The Value-Sales Differential" by Victor J. Cook, Jr.

Proposes a risk-adjusted measure of the difference between a firm's capitalized value and its share of net sales revenue, based on financial statements of 100 firms in five markets.

03-110 "Long-term Performance Impact of New Products and Promotions in the Auto Industry" by Koen Pauwels, Jorge Silva-Risso, Shuba Srinivasan, and Dominique M. Hanssens

Uses time-series analyses to investigate the impact of new product introductions on revenue, income, and stock market performance in the auto industry; examines the impact of promotional incentives and compares with effects of new product introductions.

03-111 "Which Marketing Metrics Are Used and Where?" by Patrick Barwise and John U. Farley

Reports findings of a study of leading marketing firms in the U.S., U.K., Germany, Japan, and France.

03-112 "Using Customer Lifetime Value in Customer Selection and Resource Allocation" by Rajkumar Venkatesan and V. Kumar

Analyzes customer lifetime value as a metric for identifying profitable customers and compares to other customer-selection metrics; develops CLV-based model for optimizing marketing communications.

03-115 "Should Firms Increase Advertising Expenditures during Recessions?" by Kristina D. Frankenberger and Roger C. Graham

Assesses the effects of changes in advertising spending during a recession on financial performance and firm value; compares consumer products, industrial products, and service industries.

03-123 "Assessing the Impact of Dedicated New Product Development Resources on Firm Return on Investment by David H. Henard, M. Ann McFadyen, and Keven C. Malkewitz

Uses a longitudinal approach (22 firms over seven years) to examine the relationship between dedicated human and financial resources and return on investment

03-126 "Branding Strategy and the Intangible Value of the Firm" by Vithala R. Rao, Manoj K. Agarwal, and Denise Dahlhoff

Examines branding strategies in 113 U.S. firms to determine which of three strategies (corporate branding, house of brands, or mixed branding) is associated with higher values of Tobin's q for the firm.

03-500 "Measuring and Allocating Marcom Budgets: Seven Expert Points of View" edited by Rajeev Batra and David Reibstein

Joint report of MSI and the University of Michigan's Yaffe Center for Persuasive Communication; includes seven perspectives on how companies might think through the challenge of how to use marketing communication resources most effectively.

04-102 "Market-based Assets and Capabilities, Business Processes, and Financial Performance" by Sridhar N. Ramaswami, Mukesh Bhargava, and Rajendra Srivastava

Develops a framework to show how marketing contributes to business performance by bringing market-based assets and capabilities to bear on three business processes: new product development, customer relationship management, and supply chain management.

04-103 "The Difference Between Perceptual and Objective Performance Measures: An Empirical Analysis" by Kusum L. Ailawadi, Rajiv P. Dant, and Dhruv Grewal

Investigates the effects of difference sources of common method variance in a study of channel performance; uses subjective and objective performance measures to separate the influence of measurement instrument format and response styles from respondents' psychological processes.

04-105 "Are Physicians 'Easy Marks'? Quantifying the Effects of Detailing and Sampling on New Prescriptions" by Natalie Mizik and Robert Jacobson

Examines the effect of the pharmaceutical practices of detailing (sales representatives visiting physicians' offices) and sampling (providing free drug samples) on physicians' prescribing behavior.

04-110 "Advertising Spending and Market Capitalization" by Amit Joshi and Dominique M. Hanssens

With 10 years of monthly data for five PC manufacturers, uses multivariate time-series methods to examine the long-run and short-run effects, as well as the direct and indirect effects, of advertising on firm valuation.

04-603 "Assessing Marketing Strategy Performance" edited by Christine Moorman and Donald R. Lehmann

Offers a powerful set of tools—from stock return response modeling to historical analysis—to help researchers investigate how marketing influences firm performance.

05-111 "How Brand Attributes Drive Financial Performance" by Natalie Mizik and Robert Jacobson

Develops a stock return response model that links changes in brand assets to accounting performance and stock market valuation.

05-115 "Leveraging Relationship Marketing Strategies for Better Performance: A Meta-analysis" by Robert W. Palmatier, Rajiv P. Dant, Dhruv Grewal, and Kenneth R. Evans

Conducts a meta-analysis of empirical research to determine which relationship marketing strategies are most effective, under what conditions RM strategies reliably produce positive performance outcomes, and the role of mediators such as trust, commitment, and relationship quality.

05-121 "Selecting Valuable Customers Using a Customer Lifetime Value Framework" by Rajkumar Venkatesan, V. Kumar, and Timothy Bohling

Examines the ROI implications of using the customer lifetime value (CLV) metric as compared to other customer metrics; develops a methodology for optimal marketing resource allocation.

05-200 "Research Overviews" edited by Leigh McAlister

Collected papers resulting from MSI "Research Generation Workshop" in Atlanta, May 13–14, 2004. Includes overviews of research on advertising response, brands and branding, customer metrics, marketing organizations, marketing metrics, and innovation.

05-301 "Does Marketing Measure Up? Performance Metrics: Practices and Impacts" prepared by Hernan A. Bruno, Unmish Parthasarathi, and Nisha Singh

Summarizes the proceedings of the conference, "Does Marketing Measure Up? Performance Metrics: Practices and Impacts," co-sponsored by the Marketing Science Institute and the Centre for Marketing, London Business School held June 21–22, 2004 in London.

06-100 "Myopic Marketing Management: The Phenomenon and Its Long-term Impact on Firm Value" by Natalie Mizik and Robert Jacobson

Examines managers' use of short-term-oriented marketing strategies (i.e., cutting marketing expenditures) in order to inflate quarterly earnings and meet other short-term goals; analyzes long-term effects on firm value in the context of SEOs (seasoned equity offerings).

06-101 "Brand Portfolio Strategy and Firm Performance" by Neil A. Morgan and Lopo Leotte do Rego

In a study of 149 companies, examines how brand portfolio characteristics (scope, positioning, and competition) affect a firm's financial performance and marketing effectiveness and efficiency.

06-110 "Product Innovations, Advertising Spending, and Stock Returns" by Shuba Srinivasan, Koen Pauwels, Jorge Silva-Risso, and Dominique M. Hanssens

Uses large-scale econometric analysis of the automobile industry to see how customer value creation (i.e., new product introductions) and customer value communications (i.e., advertising spending) lift stock returns by improving future cash flows.

06-112 "Lifetime Value Prediction at Early Customer Relationship Stages" by Florian v. Wangenheim

Based on study of major European airline, develops a model that predicts number of transactions per period, upgrading behavior, and customer lifetime value.

06-113 "Beware the Silver Metric: Marketing Performance Measurement Has to Be Multidimensional" by Tim Ambler and John Roberts

Argues that no single metric can adequately summarize marketing performance, and examines three current approaches: return on investment, discounted cash flow metrics, and return on customer.

06-114 "Response to Ambler and Robert's 'Beware the Silver Metric'" by Don Peppers and Martha Rogers

Responds to "Beware the Silver Metric" (06-113) and discusses the advantages of Return on Customer^{sm} as a marketing metric.

06-115 "A Word of Warning Clarified: Reactions to Peppers and Rogers' Response" by Tim Ambler and John Roberts

Responds to Peppers and Rogers' commentary (06-114).

06-119 "The Impact of Market-induced versus Word-of-Mouth Customer Acquisition on Customer Equity" by Julian Villanueva, Shijin Yoo, and Dominique Hanssens

Develops a model to measure the impact of an additional customer on a firm's customer equity; compares the effects of marketing-induced versus spontaneous acquisition channels.